Henry George Madan

Lessons in elementary Dynamics

Henry George Madan

Lessons in elementary Dynamics

ISBN/EAN: 9783743343559

Manufactured in Europe, USA, Canada, Australia, Japa

Cover: Foto ©ninafisch / pixelio.de

Manufactured and distributed by brebook publishing software (www.brebook.com)

Henry George Madan

Lessons in elementary Dynamics

LESSONS IN ELEMENTARY DYNAMICS

ARRANGED BY

H. G. MADAN, M.A.

FELLOW OF QUEEN'S COLLEGE, OXFORD; ASSISTANT MASTER
IN ETON COLLEGE

'Omnia mutantur, nihil interit.'
OVID.

W. & R. CHAMBERS
LONDON AND EDINBURGH
1886

Edinburgh:
Printed by W. & R. Chambers.

PREFACE.

It seems to be pretty generally agreed that some branch of Physics should form an early, if not the very earliest part of a scientific education, involving, as it does, an examination of those general and fundamental properties which all kinds of matter possess to a greater or less extent, and by which we recognise things as being forms of matter. Of the various branches into which Physics is divided, Mechanics has an undoubted claim to the first place, from the simplicity and exactness of its laws, the readiness with which they can be demonstrated, and the multitude of practical illustrations of them which meet us on every side in the ordinary movements of life, in games, and in work. The study of Chemistry or of Electricity may be more amusing and attractive on account of the brilliant experiments associated with it, but the exact explanation of chemical and electrical phenomena is far less easy and far less certain than that of mechanical laws, and is, indeed, hardly within the grasp of minds previously untrained in scientific methods and ideas.*

An endeavour is made in this book to explain some of the properties of matter, Newton's Laws of Motion, and the modern conceptions of Energy and Work, in such a manner as involves only the most elementary knowledge of mathematics. A boy's mind is eminently practical; he is not at once struck with the force and beauty of such expressions as $S = \frac{1}{2}gt^2$ or $W = mv^2/2$; he is apt to get bewildered by, and to fail to take in, abstract mathematical demonstrations such as most elementary books take a too early opportunity of putting before him. Things cannot at first be presented to his mind in too concrete a form: illustrations drawn from the phenomena of every-day life, and the games which he enjoys, add a vigour and interest to his

* Chemistry and Electricity will probably themselves, at no very distant period, be brought under the head of branches of Dynamics.

work such as may be wanting when he is set down to calculate wearily the present value in farthings of a million dollars put out at compound interest about the date of the Flood, or to find how many square yards of paper are required to cover Westminster Hall. But he begins to think that there is 'something in it,' when he finds that in all his movements, in walking, cricket, fives, rowing, racing, &c., he is (unconsciously, it may be, but none the less really) obeying a few very simple Laws of Motion, and that even these are little more than an expansion of the great principle of Energy.

Further, a beginner wants precise definitions of terms, and cannot easily pick out what he wants from such casual mention or diffuse explanation of them as appears sufficient to many writers. An attempt is here made to give shortly and exactly the real scientific meaning of such expressions as 'above,' 'below,' 'on the same level,' 'out of the perpendicular,' 'weighing' things; and from the same motive the Laws of Motion are divided into short statements which are considered separately.

It was at first intended that the book should be a new edition of the small treatise on the *Laws of Matter and Motion*, issued by the same publishers; but examination soon showed that most of the treatise could not fairly be brought into accordance with modern scientific ideas. A few paragraphs of it have, however, been made use of, with more or less alteration.

No originality whatever is claimed for this treatise; its aim being simply to put useful, thought-suggesting facts in a plain, straightforward way.

H. G. MADAN.

ETON COLLEGE, *August* 1886.

It has been very reluctantly decided not to introduce the Metric System into this issue of the book. An account of the system is given in the Appendix, and any opinions as to the advisability of using it in a future edition (if called for), will be gratefully received.

CONTENTS.

PAGE

Chapter I.—General Properties of Matter.

Section 1.	The Scope of Natural Science	5
„ 2.	Extension and Form	8
„ 3.	Impenetrability	8
„ 4.	States of Aggregation	9
„ 5.	Divisibility.	11
„ 6.	Indestructibility	13
„ 7.	Porosity	14
„ 8.	Attractability	15
„ 9.	Cohesion	16
„ 10.	Adhesion	21
„ 11.	Capillarity—Diffusion—Osmose	23
„ 12.	Gravitation	29
„ 13.	Mass and Weight	35
„ 14.	Density	36

Chapter II.—Motion—Force—Momentum.

Section 1.	Motion and Velocity	38
„ 2.	Force	39
„ 3.	Momentum	41
„ 4.	Measurement of Forces	42
	Appendix.—Problems on Momentum	43

Chapter III.—Laws of Motion.

Section 1.	The First Law of Motion	45
„ 2.	Laws of Centrifugal Tendency	51
„ 3.	Friction	57
„ 4.	The Second Law of Motion	65
„ 5.	Composition of Forces	68
„ 6.	Resolution of Forces	73
	Appendix.—Action of the Rudder of a Ship	76
Section 7.	The Third Law of Motion	77
„ 8.	Collision of Bodies	80
„ 9.	Laws of Reflexion	83
	Appendix	85

Chapter IV.—Acceleration.

		PAGE
Section 1.	General Principles	87
" 2.	Gravitation as an Accelerating Force	88

Chapter V.—Centre of Gravity.

Section 1.	General Principles	95
" 2.	Equilibrium of Bodies	96
" 3.	Methods of finding the Centre of Gravity	106
	Appendix.—Centre of Percussion or of Inertia	110

Chapter VI.—Energy and Work.

Section 1.	General Principles	111
" 2.	Statical and Kinetic Energy	112
" 3.	Conservation of Energy	115
" 4.	Measurement of Energy	116
	Appendix A.—Exact Valuation of the Energy in a moving body	121
	Appendix B.—The Pendulum	122

Chapter VII.—Machines.

Section 1.	General Principles	128
	Mechanical Advantage	130
" 2.	Pulleys	131
" 3.	The Wheel and Axle	135
" 4.	The Lever	140
" 5.	The Inclined Plane	148
" 6.	The Locomotive Engine as an illustration of the Principles of Dynamics	154

Appendix—The Metric System of Measures and Weights	158
Questions and Exercises	164
Index	177

LESSONS IN ELEMENTARY DYNAMICS.

CHAPTER I.

GENERAL PROPERTIES OF MATTER.

SECTION 1.—THE SCOPE OF NATURAL SCIENCE.

1. As we look around us at the vast crowd of objects which our senses make us aware of, and which make up what we call 'nature,' or the 'natural world,' we cannot help being struck by two things; firstly, the immense variety of these 'phenomena' as they are termed (Greek φαινόμενα, appearances); and secondly, the ceaseless changes which they are undergoing. No one can help asking what these objects really are, watching their various actions on one another, and trying to find out the reasons of what he sees. And no one can study nature carefully without becoming convinced that the universe is not a mere collection of things brought together by accident and ruled by chance, but that there is an *order* throughout it; that one thing happens *because* something else has previously happened; in a word, that every particular change is the effect of some definite cause. Thus, the boiling of water is an effect of which the cause is heat. But we are at once led on to inquire what is the cause of the heat itself; and thus we trace back a phenomenon through a long series of effects and causes, all connected together like the links of a chain.

2. When we have found out an unchangeable link of connection between two or more phenomena, we are said to have

discovered or established a *law* of nature. It is observed, for instance, that whenever matter is heated, it becomes enlarged in bulk; it is therefore recorded as a law of nature, that 'heat expands bodies.'

3. When, again, we can show that some other phenomenon, seemingly widely different, is really, though indirectly, caused by the operation of the same law, we are said to *explain* that phenomenon. Thus we explain the fact that a clock is apt to go slower in summer than in winter, by first establishing that a clock goes slower the longer the pendulum is, and then inferring from the law of expansion by heat, that the pendulum must be longer in summer than in winter; so that the alteration in rate is accounted for by the difference in temperature of the seasons. The knowledge of these natural laws or rules according to which the manifold changes going on in the universe seem to occur, constitutes natural science in its widest sense. But although we know, as yet, very little of what might be known about the laws of nature, still the range of even our present knowledge is so extensive that no one mind can take it all in. Hence natural science is divided into a number of departments or branches, each relating to a particular set of the phenomena which occur in nature.

4. Some phenomena depend upon the peculiar kind of substance of which the body manifesting them is composed, and consist in permanent changes in appearance and properties; as when sulphur, at a certain temperature, takes fire—that is, unites with the oxygen of the atmosphere, and forms a suffocating gas, totally unlike either sulphur or oxygen. The study of facts of this class forms the branch of science called **Chemistry**.

5. Organised bodies—that is, plants and animals—also manifest a peculiar set of appearances which are summed up in the word *life*. The consideration of *vital* phenomena belongs to the department of science called **Biology**.

6. But there is a large and important class of phenomena of a much less special kind, and which belong to matter in general and to all bodies composed of it, whatever be their peculiar constitution, and whether organic or inorganic. Thus, a stone, a piece of sulphur, a plant, an animal, all fall to the earth if unsupported, are all capable of being expanded by heat,

all reflect more or less light, &c. It is the investigation of universal laws of this kind, where no change of constitution is concerned, that forms the branch of natural science called **Physics**.

7. Of those physical phenomena, again, some have a higher generality than others, and it is these most general laws of the material world that naturally form the subject of this introductory treatise. Thus, every kind of matter is found to be capable of being altered in shape, or moved, when a sufficient amount of some power or force is applied to it. The study of the effect of forces in producing motion of masses of matter constitutes the branch of Physics called **Dynamics**.

8. Matter (Lat. *materies*), which may be defined as the material or stuff of which things are made, has certain **properties**; by which is meant, that it has the power of making certain impressions upon our senses, or of exciting in us *sensations*. Through these sensations we are said to have a *perception* of matter and bodies; but as to what matter is in itself, beyond its power of affecting our senses, we know nothing. The something, whatever it is, in which this power is conceived to reside, is called *substance*. Some philosophers deny the existence of anything beyond the properties; but though we have no direct evidence of anything else, it is difficult, if not impossible, to get rid of the notion, that there is a substance to which the properties belong. So far as natural science is affected, the question is of no moment; what really concerns us is, how matter appears and acts, and not what it is.

9. The more important of the properties of matter are— Extension, Impenetrability, Divisibility, Inertia, Porosity, Attraction, States of Aggregation, &c. We shall describe and illustrate them in succession, classing such qualities together as seem to be naturally connected. Extension and Impenetrability claim precedence as being essential to our very notion of a body. We cannot conceive a body that does not extend over or occupy a portion of space, however small, and that does not exclude all other bodies from occupying the same space while it is there. This quality of obstinately shutting out other portions of matter from its own room, seems really what we chiefly mean by substance.

Section 2.—Extension and Form.

10. Magnitude or size is one of those simple ideas that do not require or admit of explanation, because there is nothing simpler to explain them by. It is chiefly by their occupying a certain amount of space that bodies make themselves known to our senses; and when we try to think of those minute particles of matter that elude the senses, we must still conceive them as being extended or having a certain magnitude.

11. Bodies are extended in three directions, or have three *dimensions*—namely, length, breadth, and depth. Width is the same dimension as breadth; and for depth we often use the term height, and sometimes thickness. The way in which these dimensions are bounded gives each body its peculiar form or shape. This is equally true of a block of stone, a sheet of paper, a hair, a particle of dust.

12. In a line we consider only length, or linear magnitude; and the quantity of it is expressed in numbers of some convenient unit, as an inch, a foot, a metre.* In a surface we consider both length and breadth, or superficial magnitude. This, which is sometimes called *area*, is expressed in *square* inches, *square* feet, *square* metres, &c. Solid magnitude has length, breadth, and depth. The quantity of solid magnitude in any body makes its size, bulk, or *volume*; and is expressed in *cubic* inches, *cubic* metres, &c.

13. *Surfaces* are the boundaries of solid and liquid bodies, and *lines* are the boundaries of surfaces. Thus, an ordinary box is bounded by six plane surfaces, and these surfaces are bounded or separated from one another by lines or edges. A sphere is bounded by one *curved* surface.

Section 3.—Impenetrability.

14. *Impenetrability* is that quality of bodies by virtue of which each occupies a certain portion of space, to the exclusion of all other bodies: it expresses the fact that two bodies cannot be in the same place at the same time. The term Impenetrability is not a happy one, though it is difficult to find a better.

---
* An account of the metric system of measures and weights is given at the end of the book.

In the popular sense of the word, matter is anything but impenetrable. The hand can be thrust into water, a nail can be driven into wood, and even the hardest substances are pierced by others that are more or equally hard. But all these are instances merely of displacement, or of removing part of one body to make room for another. There is no wood where the nail is, nor are the particles of the removed wood driven into one another, so to speak; they are merely forced closer together, as those of a sponge are when squeezed. In some cases it might seem at first sight that something like interpenetration of substances actually takes place. Water will rise in vapour, and yet the portion of air in which it disappears may not occupy more room than it did before. A measure of water and one of sulphuric acid mixed together, occupy less space than the two did separately. But in such cases we must conceive the particles of the one substance as finding room in the intervals between the particles of the other, as will be more fully spoken of under Divisibility and Porosity.

15. That the most movable and unsubstantial substances, when displacement is prevented, occupy space as effectually as the most solid, is seen in a blown bladder, or in an air-cushion. This property of air is taken advantage of in the diving-bell. An easy illustration is obtained by pressing a common glass tumbler, mouth downwards, into a vessel of water. Though the water ascends more or less according to the depth, the air makes good its claim at ordinary depths to the greater part of the space, and even though sunk to the bottom of the sea, the water would never get quite to the top. If a small lighted taper, floating on a bit of cork, be carried down with the tumbler, the singular appearance may be beheld of a light burning under water.

Section 4.—States of Aggregation.

16. Matter is found to exist in three states or conditions, namely—

Solid, as iron, stone, ice.
Liquid,* as water, spirit of wine, mercury.
Gaseous,* as air, steam, coal-gas, chlorine (a gas which is

* 'Fluid' is a term which includes both liquids and gases.

remarkable as not being colourless like most gases, but bright yellowish green, and having a strong smell).

17. We recognise these states by the following characteristics.

(*a*) A **solid** has a definite shape and size, which it does not change unless some force is used. All its surfaces are clearly and sharply defined, as we see in the case of a brick, a bar of iron, a piece of ice. This regularity of shape is beautifully shown in crystals, such as those which are deposited when a hot strong solution of alum is allowed to cool, and the various kinds of spar which are found lining cavities in rocks. The surfaces of these crystals are absolutely flat, and the angles at which the surfaces are inclined to each other are mathematically exact; more so than any artificial process of grinding or cutting could secure.

(*b*) A **liquid** shows little tendency to preserve any definite shape under ordinary conditions (when, however, it is not in contact with any solid, as a falling rain-drop, it shows a spherical shape), but always moulds itself to the shape of the solid vessel which contains it. It may, however, show a distinct boundary or surface at the top, as water does in an open basin or in a bottle which it only partially fills; and in this case the surface is always exactly level.

(*c*) A **gas** has no definite shape or size at all; it does not even show a level upper surface like a liquid. Matter in the state of gas manifests an extraordinary power of spreading through space, even when there is another gas in the region already. Thus if only a little chlorine is put into a bottle, it quickly spreads over the whole bottle, and, if the mouth is open, it escapes from the bottle and can in a few minutes be detected by its smell in every part of the room or house. No limit can be assigned to this power of spreading (or 'diffusion,' as it is called) of a gas; and the presence of air in the bottle or room only affects the rate at which the gas travels outwards, and not the distance or amount of diffusion. The reasons for these differences between solids, liquids, and gases, will be more easily understood when we have considered some of the other properties of matter.

Section 5.—Divisibility.

18. We are able, by mechanical means, such as cutting or pounding, to divide masses of matter into very small parts. A chip of marble may be broken from a block, and that chip may be crushed to powder. The smallest particle of this powder discernible by the naked eye, when examined by the microscope, is seen to be a block having all the qualities of the original marble, and capable, by finer instruments, of being divided into still smaller blocks, which may be again divided; and so on, with no other practical limit than the fineness of our senses and instruments.

19. Gold can be beaten out into leaves which are not more than $\frac{1}{300000}$ of an inch in thickness, and which, when placed edgeways, are quite invisible under the best microscopes hitherto made. In preparing the gilt silver wire used in embroidery, a rod of silver is covered with a thin layer of gold, and then drawn out into a fine wire, in which the thickness of the gold covering retains the same proportion to the silver as at first. A portion of this wire, on which the layer of gold is less than 1-millionth of an inch in thickness, may be seen under the microscope to be covered with a continuous coating of the metal, having all the appearance of solid gold.

20. It is possible, however, to divide matter into even smaller particles without difficulty. When a soap-bubble is blown, the solution of soap can be extended until its thickness is not greater than $\frac{1}{300000}$ of an inch before it breaks; and yet there must obviously be in this soap-film at least one row of particles of soap lying side by side thus, ooooooooo. Moreover, chemistry teaches us that each particle of soap must contain more than 50 separate particles of carbon, hydrogen, oxygen, and sodium.

21. Still more minute must be the division when a substance is dissolved in a liquid, or is heated until it assumes the state of gas. Thus when water is, by the application of heat, turned into steam, we separate it into particles far too small to be seen under any microscope, and which there are good reasons for believing to be at any rate not greater than $\frac{1}{300000000}$ of an inch in diameter.

22. Divisibility thus extends far beyond the limits perceptible to the senses. Are we therefore to assume that it is without limits—that matter is infinitely divisible? This would be a rash assumption. On the contrary, there are many reasons for believing that there is a limit somewhere, and that there are ultimate particles, of a determinate size and shape, incapable of further subdivision. Thus, in the case of steam above mentioned, it is pretty certain that we are dealing with the smallest separate particles of water that can exist at all, retaining the properties of water. These ultimate particles of matter are called **Molecules** (Lat. *molecula*, a small mass).

23. The size and shape of these molecules can only be approximately judged of by our present means; but several perfectly independent lines of research point to the following conclusions:

(a) That the molecules of all kinds of matter are spherical in shape and are all of the same size, but differ in other properties, for example, weight.

(b) That the diameter of a molecule is not greater than $\frac{1}{3000000}$ of an inch, and not much less than $\frac{1}{30000000}$ of an inch ($\frac{1}{800000} - \frac{1}{8000000}$ of a millimetre).

24. Molecules are the smallest particles recognised and dealt with in Physics; and we shall see that a great many of the peculiarities of matter can be explained by assuming their existence. But even these molecules can generally be divided by chemical means into still smaller particles, which seem to be really the smallest particles of a substance which can show the properties and affinities of the substance at all. These ultimate particles of matter are called **atoms** (from a Greek word, ἄτομος, *atomos*, signifying 'indivisible'). For example, the molecule of water can be undoubtedly separated into at least two dissimilar parts, which we call the elements 'oxygen' and 'hydrogen' respectively; such atoms of oxygen and hydrogen being incapable of existing free and uncombined, but capable of forming, with other atoms, molecules of chemical compounds.

25. The distinction, then, between a molecule of matter and an atom of matter must be carefully borne in mind.

A **molecule** is the smallest particle of matter which can exist free and uncombined.

An atom is the smallest particle of matter which can take part in a chemical combination.

SECTION 6.—INDESTRUCTIBILITY.

26. Whatever views may be taken as to the size and shape of the ultimate particles of matter, we know that human agency can neither make nor destroy them. This is not, indeed, what a first impression suggests, for nothing is more common than for bodies to decay, dissolve, evaporate, and disappear. But it can be proved that in no case is anything lost. The structure or form is destroyed, the materials remain. Water, mercury, and many other substances disappear in invisible vapour when heated; but if the vapour is carefully collected and cooled, the water or mercury reappears without loss of weight.

27. When a piece of wood is heated in a close vessel from which air is excluded, we obtain water, an acid, several kinds of gas, and there remains a black, porous substance, called charcoal. The wood is thus decomposed, and its particles take a new arrangement and assume new forms; but that nothing is lost is proved by the fact, that if the water, acid, gases, and charcoal be collected and weighed, they will be found exactly as heavy as the wood was before distillation. In the same manner, the substance of the coal burnt in our fires is not annihilated; it is only dispersed in the form of smoke or particles of soot, gas, and ashes or dust. Bones, flesh, and other animal substances may in the same manner be made to assume new forms, without the destruction of a particle of the matter which they originally contained. The decay of animal or vegetable bodies in the open air, or in the ground, is only a process by which the atoms of which they were composed change their places, and enter into new combinations.

28. It is equally true that matter cannot be made or called into existence by us. We talk of 'making' a chair, but this really means only putting into a new shape matter which already exists. Every particle of the matter of which we ourselves, our flesh and bones, are made, existed already in the food we eat. The plants on which we feed, and on which the animals thrive,

which we also use as food, derive their materials from the soil, air, and water, which surround them; and the decay and decomposition of animal and vegetable matter after death supply the materials for another generation of animals and plants. The universe, in fact, so far as we know, contains precisely the same number and kind of atoms of matter that it had when it was created, and neither more nor fewer.

Section 7.—Porosity.

29. In common language, a pore (Greek πόρος, a path) is a small hollow space or interstice between the particles of a body, large enough to be seen, or to admit the passage of liquids or gases. In this sense, some substances, such as sponge, charcoal, sugar, &c., are called *porous*, and others are contrasted with them as *solid*. But experiment and reflection lead us to the conclusion that all bodies are porous—that is, that in no case do the molecules fill the whole space occupied by the body, but that there are, even in the most *solid* of solids, interstices of greater or less size between them.

30. In the first place, liquids and gases are found to pass through what seem the most compact solids. If a wooden cask full of spirits of wine is sunk in water for a time, the cask will be found filled with water, and the spirits gone. The spirits escape, and the water enters through the pores of the wood. A globe of silver filled with water, and closed with a screw, was once submitted to great pressure; the surface of the metal became covered with dew, the water being forced through its pores. In using Bramah's hydraulic presses, in which water is forced under great pressure into cast-iron or steel cylinders four or five inches thick, the water is often observed to pass through the pores of the metal, and stand out like drops of dew on its surface. Similarly gases, especially hydrogen gas, are found to pass pretty readily through heated plates of platinum and iron.

31. In the next place, when a substance is placed under heavy pressure, or cooled, it contracts in volume—that is, its molecules get nearer to each other; and this could not occur unless there were already spaces between them. Gases are thus shown to be extremely porous. Air has been compressed into less than $\frac{1}{1000}$

of the space it usually occupies, without reaching the limit of its compressibility. Again, if water is allowed to evaporate in a closed vessel 'filled' (as we usually say) with air, just as much water-vapour is formed in the vessel as if there was no air already in it. And if ether is now introduced into the vessel and vaporised, just as much of its vapour is formed as if the vessel contained no water-vapour or air already, the only difference being that a longer time is required, the fresh molecules having to fight their way through an already somewhat crowded space. We may go on putting into the same vessel other vapours to an extent of which the limit has not yet been found; so large are the intervals between the molecules of gases at ordinary temperatures and pressures.*

Section 8.—Attractability.

32. The term 'attraction,' by which we express simply the tendency of one thing to approach another, is applied to a great many phenomena which we must regard as due to different causes. The tendency which is shown by a stone to fall to the earth, is an example of an attraction due to the force of **Gravitation**. The particles of the stone are held together by an attraction called **Cohesion**; and mortar sticks to the stone in consequence of a very similar attraction called **Adhesion**.

[Other kinds of attraction are **Magnetic attraction**, which is manifested between a piece of iron and a magnet, and between certain parts of two magnets; **Electrical attraction**, which occurs between a piece of glass when rubbed with silk, for instance, and other substances; and **Chemical attraction**, which enables atoms (and not merely molecules) to associate closely and form definite, permanent chemical compounds, as when the elements oxygen and hydrogen unite to form water. But the study of these special attractive forces belongs to other branches of natural science, and will not be further pursued here.]

---

* Of course, the addition of each successive gas increases the pressure on the internal surface of the vessel, as more and more molecules are crowded in.

It may be interesting to note that in one cubic inch of air, at ordinary temperatures and pressures, there are probably 300,000,000,000,000,000,000 molecules of oxygen and nitrogen. In one cubic centimetre, the size of one side of which is here given, there are 2,000,000,000,000,000,000 molecules of a gas.

Fig. 1.

Section 9.—Cohesion.

33. This is the name given (from Lat. *cohærere*, to stick together) to the attractive force which holds together molecules of the same kind, so as to form masses or bodies of matter. Without such a force we should not have a compact mass of sandstone, but a mere loose heap of sand; steel would not be a substance hard enough to cut most other things, but a mass as weak and unstable as water.

34. Cohesion acts only when the molecules are at distances so minute as to be insensible to us: at distances greater than $\frac{1}{500000}$ of an inch, it has no influence whatever; and when the molecules of a solid body are once separated, it is in most cases impossible to bring them near enough again to make them cohere. Two fresh cut surfaces of lead may be made to cohere with some force; but a slight film of rust or of grease will completely prevent the necessary nearness of the metallic molecules. Interrupted cohesion is easily restored when the body is in a fluid or half-fluid state, owing to the mobility of the molecules; as when a broken stick of sealing-wax is mended by melting the two ends and pressing them together, or two pieces of iron are joined by welding.

35. The difference between the three states of matter, solid, liquid, and gaseous, already treated of in par. 17, page 10, can be explained as due to differences in the extent to which cohesion is allowed to exert its power in holding the molecules together.

36. In **solids**, cohesion shows itself strongly; the molecules are held firmly together, and can only be separated or altered in relative position by a considerable force. Hence a solid is observed to keep its shape.

37. In **liquids**, cohesion scarcely shows itself at all: the molecules move easily past one another, and are easily separated entirely. Hence the weight of the molecules is free to act, and presses them into all the irregularities of shape of the vessel containing them, as if into a mould: it also causes them all to get as near the earth's centre as they can, a condition which can only be satisfied by the upper surface of the liquid (that is, that

farthest from the earth's centre) being perfectly level. Hence also each drop of a liquid is perfectly spherical in shape.

38. In **gases**, no cohesion at all is shown : the molecules are believed to be in extremely rapid motion, darting about in all directions in straight lines, and knocking continually against one another, and against whatever resists their onward course. Hence there is a constant pressure against the sides of the vessel which contains them, and a tendency of the gas to escape in whatever direction the movements of the molecules are freest; for example, through the mouth of the bottle, in whatever direction it may be turned. This view of the nature of gases is called the **Kinetic Theory** (from a Greek word, *κίνησις,* movement); and it completely explains nearly all the observed facts.*

39. It is found that by simply applying heat to a substance, we can change its state from solid to liquid and from liquid to gaseous. Ice, for instance, when heated, becomes water; and when further heated, the water turns into steam. Similarly, by taking away heat, and nothing else, from a gas, it assumes successively the liquid and solid states. Hence we infer that heat is the force which counteracts cohesion in liquids and gases.

40. Some substances occur in a state which is intermediate between solid and liquid—for instance, oil, treacle, honey. In such a state they are said to be 'viscous.' They show the general characteristics of liquids, but imperfectly; issuing in a sluggish stream when poured out of a vessel, and remaining heaped up for a certain time on the surface upon which they are poured, though they eventually adapt themselves to its shape, and show a level upper surface. In them cohesion shows itself to a certain extent between the molecules, but not so much as to enable them to retain a shape permanently as a solid does.

41. The character and amount of cohesion varies greatly with the nature of the particular substance. Hence arise the manifold

---

* The quickness of the motion of the molecules of a gas is surprisingly great. The molecules of air, under ordinary conditions, are moving at the rate of 17 miles a minute. The molecules of hydrogen gas are moving even faster—that is, about 60 miles a minute, 60 times faster than an express train. This explains the ease with which gases pass through fine tubes or cracks, or through pores such as exist in unglazed earthenware (like that of which flower-pots are made).

degrees of hardness, tenacity, and elasticity, which must be more fully considered.

42. Hardness.—This means, resistance of the molecules of a mass to any change in their relative positions. When, for instance, we find that great force is required to cut into or alter the shape of a mass, as in the case of steel or glass, we call that substance 'hard.' It is the result of very strong cohesion between the molecules; and hence solids show it to a much greater extent than fluids. But even in solids hardness differs greatly (compare, for instance, glass with lead), and those substances which easily yield to force we call 'soft,' meaning only that they are less hard than the majority of substances. Softness is, in fact, merely a comparative term; just as in calling a thing cold, we simply mean that it is less hot than other things with which we compare it.

43. We can easily find out which of two things is the hardest by trying which will make a scratch or groove in the other. The one which does so—that is, which displaces the molecules of the other—must have the stronger cohesion, and therefore must be the harder. From results of experiments of this kind, it is easy to make out such a list as the following, in which the substances are arranged in order of hardness. Each is scratched by those above it in the list, but will scratch all those below it.

1. Diamond (the hardest substance known).
2. Quartz (rock-crystal or flint).
3. Glass.
4. Steel.*
5. Iron.
6. Copper.
7. Lead.
8. Wax.
9. Butter.

The substances in the second column we should call, as a rule, 'soft'; but it must be repeated that there is no definite line to be drawn where hardness ends and softness begins.

44. A hard substance is generally very **brittle**—that is, the cohesion acts only through a very small distance, and its molecules cannot be moved far from their positions without passing beyond the range of their cohesive force, and breaking apart. A

---

* See par. 50, note.

diamond can readily be crushed to powder by blows of a hammer; glass is an almost proverbial example of brittleness, and a file of hardened steel sometimes snaps in two when simply allowed to fall on a stone floor.

45. **Tenacity** (Lat. *tenax, tenere,* to hold).—This means resistance of the molecules to complete separation, even when their places are greatly changed by force: cohesion acting through a longer range than in the case of brittle substances. It is a quality shown chiefly by substances which are only moderately hard, such as ordinary steel, iron, and brass. Such substances can be bent, twisted, hammered out into thin plates (**malleability**), pulled out into fine wire (**ductility**), and will sustain great pressure (or 'stress,' as it is scientifically termed) without breaking; hence they are of great use for engineering purposes.

46. Tenacity is usually measured by hanging weights from a rod of the substance, and observing what force is required to tear it in two. A table of the 'breaking stress,' as it is called, of a few substances is given below—

Breaking stress of a wire $\frac{1}{10}$ of an inch in diameter:

Steel	1000 lbs.	Copper	300 lbs.
Iron (wrought)	550 "	Gold	150 "
Brass	470 "	Lead	25 "

47. The malleability of some of the metals is remarkable. In the manufacture of 'gold leaf' for gilding purposes, a bar of gold is first rolled out between polished rollers into a ribbon about $\frac{1}{1000}$ of an inch in thickness. This is cut into small squares, which are placed between sheets of vellum and beaten out with heavy hammers. The extended leaves are then cut into smaller pieces, and the latter are beaten out between sheets of a thin membrane called 'gold-beater's skin'; and the process is repeated until leaves are obtained about $3\frac{1}{2}$ inches square and not more than $\frac{1}{250000}$ of an inch ($\frac{1}{10000}$ of a millimetre) thick; the cohesion of the molecules enabling them to hold together even under this great extension. The leaves thus produced are actually transparent, transmitting a beautiful green light. Silver and platinum can be beaten out in a similar way into leaves nearly but not quite as thin as gold.

48. The same metals also show great ductility. Wire is made by pulling a thin rod of the metal through a conical hole in a steel plate, the smaller end of the hole being rather less in diameter than the rod. The metal is thus, partly by the pull and partly by the compression as it passes through the hole, made longer and thinner; and by drawing it through smaller and smaller holes in succession very thin wire can be obtained, the thinnest gold wire being only $\frac{1}{1250}$ of an inch ($\frac{1}{50}$ of a millimetre) in diameter.

49. **Elasticity** (Greek ἴλασις, striving).—This means the tendency of the molecules of a body to go back to their original positions when their places have been altered by force. For instance, when a piece of india-rubber is stretched, its molecules submit to be moved very far from their original places without getting beyond the range of their cohesion, although they resist this change with a force which increases with the amount of displacement. But they do not rest satisfied with their new places; continued stress has to be applied in order to keep the india-rubber stretched, and as soon as this stress is taken off, the molecules come back to their precise original places, and the piece of india-rubber resumes its old form. A similar thing happens when a straight rod of whalebone or steel is bent; the molecules on the outside of the curve are pulled farther apart, while those on the inside of the curve are pushed nearer together as shown in fig. 2. But if the displacement has not exceeded a certain amount, they all come back to their original places when the pressure is taken off.

Fig. 2.

(Compare this with the behaviour of a similar strip of lead which remains bent after the removal of the pressure, the molecules making no effort to recover their places.) It is easy to see why a thin rod may be bent farther than a thick one without breaking. The thinner a rod is, the less difference in length there is between the inside and the outside of the curve when it is bent, and hence there is less displacement of the molecules for a given amount of bending. In the rebound of an elastic ball from a flat surface, a similar thing happens. The molecules of the ball are forced inwards at the moment of contact, so that the ball is flattened there; and the effort of the molecules to recover their places drives the whole ball back.

50. The solids which show elasticity in the highest degree are india-rubber, ivory, whalebone, steel (at a certain degree of hardness)*, and glass. Glass is, until it actually breaks, the most perfectly elastic solid known. A glass ball ('a solitaire' ball will do) let fall on a smooth slab of marble,† rebounds very nearly to the height from which it was let fall. A thin thread of glass, such as 'spun glass,' may be tied into a knot, or one end may be twisted 400 or 500 times round; but it will resume its exact original figure when allowed.

51. Liquids and gases are, so far as experiments have gone, perfectly elastic. We can easily change their shape, but we cannot permanently alter it by any force whatever. The compressibility of air has been already alluded to in par. 31, p. 14, and when it is released from pressure, however intense, it is found to expand again to its exact original volume.

SECTION 10.—ADHESION.

52. This is the name given (from Lat. *adhærere*, to stick to) to the attractive force which acts (at extremely small distances only) between molecules of *different* kinds of matter; which causes, for instance, glass and sealing-wax to stick together where their surfaces are in contact. It may eventually be found to be essentially the same force as cohesion, but the effects of the two are so easily distinguishable, that it is convenient to consider them separately, and give them different names.

53. Particles of dust on an upright pane of glass, chalk-marks

---

* Steel can be obtained of very various degrees of hardness. When, in the process of manufacture, it has been allowed to cool slowly from a red heat, it is scarcely harder than iron, and shows comparatively little elasticity. If heated red-hot and suddenly cooled by being plunged into cold water, it becomes (owing to a change in molecular structure) even harder than glass. In this condition it is very brittle, and its elasticity is only shown within narrow limits. But if this hard steel is carefully heated to a definite temperature ($285°$ centigrade), and allowed to cool slowly, it is rendered less hard, and shows a very high degree of elasticity. In this state it is used for watch-springs, &c.

† A slab of glass should not be used for this experiment.

on a wall, glue on wood or paper, paint on metals, &c., are all instances of adhesion between dissimilar kinds of matter. The use of cements depends upon the adhesion of the molecules of the cementing substance to the surfaces between which it lies, and also upon the cohesion between its own molecules. When both are strong, as in the case of glue between surfaces of wood, the joint is often the strongest part of the mass; so that if two pieces of wood are well glued together and then broken, the fracture will take place anywhere rather than at the joint.*

54. Glue has, on the contrary, very slight adhesion for metals or glass, and hence it is of little use as a cement for such substances; shellac, or some other gum-resin, must be used.

55. Adhesion of liquids to solids takes place much more readily than that of solids to solids, because in the case of a liquid and a solid the surfaces come into more complete contact. When the hand or a rod of metal is dipped into water, a film of the water adheres to the surface, and is borne up against its own weight; nor can any force shake it all off. Plunge a bit of gold, or silver, or lead, into mercury, and a portion of the mercury will in like manner adhere. Wherever we have *wetting*, we have a case of adhesion of a liquid to a solid. It is from this cause that in pouring water over the edge of a vessel, the water is apt to run down the side of the vessel rather than fall perpendicularly. To avoid this, jugs, &c., have lips or spouts; the liquid, when it gets to the lower end of the lip, can only continue in contact with the glass by running uphill, along the curved under-surface of the lip, and its weight prevents it from doing this, so it falls straight off. A temporary lip may be made by

---

* A good illustration of the relation of adhesion to cohesion is afforded by the common experiment of splitting a sheet of paper in two. Take a piece of paper such as a printed leaf of a book or newspaper, and two pieces of calico rather larger than the paper. Lay the pieces of calico upon a board, and brush thin glue over them, leaving one corner or edge untouched. Place the sheet of paper between them, and press them into close contact with the paper in every part; then hang the whole up to dry. When dry, take hold of the unglued corners of the calico, and tear the two pieces slowly and carefully apart. The cohesion of the calico and the glue, and the adhesion of the glue to the calico and the paper, are both so much greater than the cohesion of the paper, that the latter will split in two, half of the thickness remaining attached to each piece of calico, from which it may be detached by soaking for a few minutes in hot water.

holding a wetted glass rod vertically against the edge of the jar or basin.

56. But liquids do not always wet solids, or adhere to them. A rod coated with grease, or the wing of a water-fowl, remains dry when plunged in water. Mercury does not adhere to a porcelain cup, or to a rod of iron or platinum. The explanation is simple. There is probably in every case an attraction between the solid surface and the liquid, but it is opposed by the attraction of the particles of the liquid for one another, and there can be actual adhesion only when the first is stronger than the other. When the adhesive force is able to overcome the attraction of the liquid for its own particles, a film of it is separated and carried off on the surface of the solid; if the cohesion of the liquid is the stronger of the two, there is no wetting of the surface.

Section 11.—Capillarity—Diffusion—Osmose.

57. Cohesion shows itself at the surface of liquids in a striking way. It causes all the molecules in the surface-layer to be in a state of strain not unlike that of a stretched sheet of india-rubber. This is called the **surface tension** of a liquid; and it is well shown in the strong tendency of a soap-bubble to contract in size, the molecules of the surface-layers dragging at each other so as to make the film shrink into the smallest possible space. Thus, if after a bubble is blown at the end of a funnel,* the mouth is withdrawn from the end of the tube before the bubble is detached, the latter begins to contract with a force sufficient to drive a strong stream of air out of the tube, as may be proved by holding the flame of a candle close to its end.

58. The surface tension of water is strong, but it is greatly weakened by contact with some other liquids. If a clean† glass plate is laid flat, and a little water is poured over it, and spread

---

* Thistle funnels with long stems, such as are used in chemical work, answer well for blowing bubbles. A good solution is made by dissolving 5 grms. of sodium oleate in 80 c.c. of distilled water, and adding 5 c.c. of glycerine, mixing the whole thoroughly.

†.The plate should be cleaned by rubbing over it a little nitric acid with a tuft of cotton wool, and then rinsing it with water.

with a glass rod so as to form a thin even layer, and if then a drop of spirit of wine on the end of a glass rod is put in the middle of the water, the surface tension is lessened at this point, and the molecules shrink away on all sides, like a retreating army, so as to form a ring round the drop, separated from it by a clear space. A drop of oil, placed on the surface of the water in a similar way, follows up the retreating molecules and spreads quickly over a large surface. Many different and curious 'cohesion-figures' may be formed by dropping various liquids, such as ether, turpentine, oil of cloves, upon a thin layer of water as above described.

59. *Capillary Attraction* is only a particular effect of cohesion and adhesion. A tube with a small bore, like a hair, is called a capillary tube, from *capillus*, the Latin word for a hair. If the end of such a glass tube is dipped in water, the water is seen to

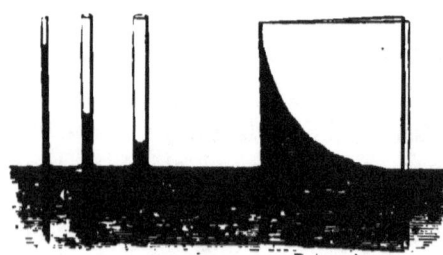

Fig. 3.

rise in the tube above the level of the rest of the surface. In a series of tubes of different diameters, the liquid ascends highest in the smallest; or the heights are inversely as the diameters. Water will be seen to rise in a similar way between two glass plates placed as in the figure, with two of the upright edges touching, and the other two slightly apart. The sustained film rises higher as the plates approach, assuming the form of a particular curve. The fluid rises also slightly on the outside of the tubes and plates, and the surface of the sustained column within the tube is seen to be hollow like a cup.

60. But liquids do not always ascend in narrow tubes or spaces; it is only when they adhere to the solid substance that they do so. If a greasy glass tube is dipped in water; or, still better, if a clean glass tube is dipped in mercury, the liquid inside, instead of rising, sinks below the general level; the surface of the column, too, becomes convex instead of concave.

61. The rise or the depression depends upon the adjustment

between the forces of adhesion and cohesion, as in the case of wetting. When the liquid wets the tube, the particles close to its surface have part of their weight supported by adhesion, and thus a longer column is required to balance the pressure of the rest of the fluid. In cases where the cohesive attraction of the liquid particles within the tube for one another is too strong to permit them to adhere to its surface, that cohesion tends to draw them away from it, while the tube prevents them from receiving the support they would have from the liquid particles around them, if it were not there. Mathematicians have shown that, if the adhesion between the solid and the liquid be equal to half the cohesion of the particles of the fluid, the surface at the point of contact will be neither elevated nor depressed; if the adhesion between the two be more than half the cohesion, elevation will occur; and if it be less than half, the surface will be depressed and convex.

62. Capillary attraction is exemplified in many familiar phenomena, and plays an important part in nature. Thus, the rise of the sap from the roots into the branches and leaves of plants is mainly due to capillary action in the numerous small tubes of which vegetable tissue is in a great measure composed. If a piece of sponge or a lump of sugar be placed so that its lower corner touches some water, the fluid will rise up and wet the whole mass. In the same manner, the wick of a lamp will carry up the oil to supply the flame, though the flame is several inches above the level of the oil. The use of blotting-paper depends on the tendency of the ink to rise by capillary attraction through the pores of the paper. If one end of a towel happens to be left in a basin of water, while the other hangs over below the level of the water, the basin will be emptied of its contents; and, on the same principle, when a dry wedge of wood is driven into the crevice of a rock, and afterwards moistened with water, it will absorb the water, swell, and sometimes split the rock.

63. A striking illustration of this subject is given by the following experiment: Place a wine-glass on a book on the table, and set another close by it, so as to be on a lower level. Pour some water and some oil into the higher glass; then moisten a piece of cotton-wick in water, and drop an end of it into each glass, so as to reach near the bottom and form a bridge between

them. The water which was below the oil in the one glass will in an hour or two be found transferred to the other, leaving the oil behind. If the wick be moistened with oil, the oil will be transferred, leaving the water.

64. When two light bodies, such as two bits of cork, are left to float on water near each other, they soon come together, moving at last with a rush. This is owing to the attraction of adhesion which we are considering. When the liquid wets the floating bodies, it rises slightly all round them, and this sustained liquid hangs as a weight on them on all sides. So long as it rises equally, there is no motion; but when the bodies come near each other, the space between them becomes like part of the inside of a capillary tube, the water rises higher than on the opposite sides, and the bodies move towards the sides that are most strongly pulled. When the floating bodies are not wetted by the liquid, the effect is the same as if there was a repulsion between them and it; the surface between the two bodies is depressed, and they are pushed together by the higher column on the outside. If one of two bodies floating on water is smeared with oil, so as to prevent the water from adhering, instead of coming together, the two will recede from each other, for reasons analogous to the above.

65. **Adhesion between Solids and Gases.**—Every solid has, under ordinary conditions, a film of air adhering to its surface, which it is extremely difficult to get rid of. Dry iron-filings, and even small needles, when gently laid on the surface of water, will float, though eight times heavier than the water, because each has a film of air adhering to it so strongly that even when it does sink it carries a portion of the air along with it. In making barometers, it is found that air adheres so firmly to the surface of the glass, that the mercury must be boiled in the tube before it can be expelled. Some porous solids, such as charcoal, absorb air and other gases to an amount many times their own bulk, the force of adhesion condensing the gases on the surface of their molecules. When a lump of sugar is dropped into a cup of tea, the film of air which surrounds the particles does not quit them till they are dissolved; bubbles are seen rising till all the sugar has disappeared.

66. **Diffusion.**—By this is meant the tendency shown by fluids

to spread into one another until a perfectly uniform mixture is obtained. It depends upon the freedom of the movements of the molecules in such bodies (their cohesion having been, as already explained, p. 17, nearly or entirely overcome by heat), and the great porosity of matter in the fluid state. Thus, in liquids, the molecules, in spite of a certain amount of cohesion still showing itself, are constantly making excursions beyond their natural boundaries, and thus spreading into a space even when containing another liquid. If a jar is half filled with a strong solution of sugar or salt coloured with ink or cochineal, to render it visible, and water be poured upon the surface (very slowly and carefully, to avoid mechanical mixing of the liquids*), the boundary between the two will be pretty sharply defined for a time, but gradually the coloured solution will rise, and finally the whole mass will become equally coloured, and an equal amount of sugar or salt will be found in every part of it. It is found that the rate of diffusion varies very much with the nature of the liquid; and that solutions of substances which readily form crystals, such as sugar or salt ('crystalloids'), diffuse far quicker than solutions of such things as gum or glue, or liquids such as oil and treacle, which have no tendency to crystallise ('colloids,' from a Greek word meaning glue).

67. In gases, diffusion goes on much more quickly than in liquids, as might be expected from the quickness of the movement of the molecules of a gas (p. 17), and the large spaces between them. The rapidity with which coal gas, escaping from a leak in a pipe, diffuses through the whole room is a good example. Heavy gases diffuse much more slowly than light ones, since their molecules are in comparatively slow movement; but the ultimate result is the same in all cases, a perfectly uniform mixture being obtained. If a jar of air is inverted over a jar of chlorine, so that their open mouths are in contact, the heavy chlorine can be seen by its colour to rise into the upper jar; and the air also, though much lighter than chlorine, passes downwards, until in a short time the

---

* It is best to float a disc of paper, with a piece of thread attached to it, upon the solution, and to pour the water gently down a glass rod or pencil upon the paper. When the jar has been filled up, the paper can be gently withdrawn by means of the thread.

proportions of chlorine and air are the same in every part of the two jars.

68. Osmose.—This term is applied to the tendency shown by fluids to diffuse even through porous solids, such as paper, unglazed earthenware, and parchment or other animal membranes. The general character of the movement is much the same as in ordinary diffusion, and crystalloids show it much more than colloids, but the results are in many cases complicated by differences of adhesion between the fluids and the surface of the solid.

69. The distinction between colloids and crystalloids is even more sharply marked in osmose than in the case of direct diffusion. If, for instance, a glass cylinder (such as a lamp glass), with a piece of parchment or bladder tied over one end, is filled with a mixture of gum and sugar dissolved in water, and hung in a basin of pure water, so that diffusion can take place through the parchment, it is found that the sugar (a crystalloid) soon passes through into the surrounding water, while practically none of the gum (a colloid) passes through at all. At the same time the water from the outer vessel passes through the membrane more quickly than the solution of sugar, owing partly to its greater adhesion to the animal tissue, and thus the liquid in the cylinder becomes increased in volume, as shown by its surface rising above its original level. This experiment illustrates a method called 'Dialysis,' which is used to separate mixtures of crystalloids and colloids.

70. In the case of gases, some curious results are obtained by the different rates at which they diffuse through a porous substance. If a wide glass tube, or lamp cylinder, closed at one end by a plug of well-dried plaster of Paris, is filled with hydrogen (or coal gas),* and placed with its open end dipping under water in a basin, the light hydrogen will pass out through the pores of the plaster so much quicker than the denser air enters, that the volume of gas in the tube will for some time be diminished, and the level of the water inside will rapidly rise much above the level of the water in the basin. If the mouth of a tumbler is dipped into solution of soap, so as to form a flat

---

* While it is being filled, the end closed by the plug should be temporarily covered by an india-rubber cap, to prevent premature diffusion.

soap film adhering to its edge, and then placed in a jar of carbon dioxide ('carbonic acid gas'), the soap film will soon become convex and expand into a bubble, showing that the carbon dioxide enters more rapidly than the air in the tumbler gets out through the film. Now this is contrary to what we should expect from the usual law, since carbon dioxide is much denser than air; but carbon dioxide is much more soluble in water than air is, and hence it dissolves at the outside of the soap-film, diffuses through the film in solution, and then diffuses from the inner surface into the tumbler.

Section 12.—Gravitation.

71. The attractive forces hitherto considered—namely, cohesion and adhesion—act only between certain kinds of matter, and through extremely small distances; moreover, they differ in amount according to the particular substance. But there is one attractive force, called **gravitation**, which acts between *all* kinds of matter, under all conditions, through very great distances, and according to one simple universal law. It is this force which causes things to show the property of 'weight,' by which is meant pressure towards the earth's centre. If we hold up a piece of iron in the hand, we observe that it presses against the hand in one definite direction, and we express this by saying that it is 'heavy,' or 'has weight.' If the support of the hand is taken away, the piece of iron moves, or 'falls,' towards the surface of the earth until some obstacle prevents its further movement. Evidently, however, its tendency to move does not cease when it has reached this point. It will fall down a well or shaft of a mine with scarcely diminished acceleration; and we have every reason to believe that, if it could, it would go on falling until it reached a point close to the centre of the earth, and that there it would cease to show any tendency to move in any particular direction; it would have no 'weight' at all.

72. Sir Isaac Newton, in 1665 A.D., was the first who gave a definite reason for the weight of matter. He was led, it is said, by observing an apple fall from the tree, to ask himself why it should move at all when detached from the tree; why it should

move to the earth instead of from it: how quickly it fell; whether a large mass fell at the same rate as a small one, and so on. He accounted for the fact of its fall by saying that there is a universal attraction between the molecules of matter, however great the distance between them; and so every molecule of the earth is attracting every molecule of the apple, and also every molecule of the apple is attracting those of the earth. The result of all these separate attractions is equivalent to one single force tending to move the apple in the direction of the centre of the earth; and when it has reached this point, it will be attracted equally in all directions by the earth's molecules, and so will show no pressure or tendency to move in any particular direction more than another.

73. But weight is only one case of the universal attraction of gravitation. Sir Isaac Newton went on to prove that a force acting according to the same laws holds the moon in its orbit round the earth, and the earth and other planets in their orbits round the sun. Even those almost immeasurably distant bodies, the stars, are in many cases found to consist of pairs of bodies ('double stars') revolving round each other, and held near each other by the same force.

Fig. 4.

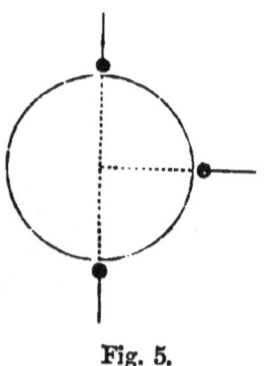

Fig. 5.

74. **Direction and Magnitude of Gravitation.**—The direction of this force, so far as relates to its action between the earth and bodies within its range, is very simply shown by hanging a weight to a string (fig. 4); the weight stretches the string in the direction in which it would fall if it could, and thus the line of the string shows the direction of gravitation at the particular place (fig. 5). This instrument is called a 'plumb-line.'

75. It will now be easy to understand the precise meaning of the common terms 'above,' 'below,' 'higher,' 'lower.' In all cases reference is made to the

earth's centre, and not necessarily to any fixed distant point in space, such as a star. When we say that a body is 'above,' or 'higher than' another, we mean that it is farther from the earth's centre, as measured along the direction of a plumb-line. When we say that it is 'below,' or 'lower than,' another body, we mean that it is nearer to the earth's centre as measured in the same way. It is in this sense that a lamp is 'above' the floor, and a dog lies 'below' or 'under' a table. Things which are at the same distance from the earth's centre are said to be at the same 'level.' If we refer the position of bodies to a fixed direction in space, such as a straight line drawn to a star, we shall see that, in the case of two bodies which are at different points along this line, the one of them which is nearest the star would be said to be 'above' the other in England, but 'below' the other in Australia, and 'on one side of' the other near the equator. But by reference to the earth's centre, the terms become perfectly definite, and have the same significance all over the world.

76. The process of weighing a thing consists in finding out how much pressure it exerts towards the earth's centre. This is usually stated by comparison with the pressure exerted by some definite piece of matter which we call a 'weight,' such as a pound or a gramme. Thus, when we say that a piece of lead weighs two pounds, we mean that it presses towards the earth's centre with twice as much force as the standard weight called a 'pound.' This comparison of weights can be made in the two following ways (among others):

(1) By placing the bodies one at each end of a rod supported at its exact centre so that it can move easily round the point of support (fig. 6); that body which pulls down its end of the rod is clearly the heavier of the two, and if the rod remains level, the bodies are of equal weight. Such an apparatus is the ordinary balance or pair of scales, a fuller account of which will be found on p. 143.

Fig. 6.

(2) By seeing how much each of the bodies will stretch a spring; the one which stretches it farthest is, of course, the heaviest. This is the principle of the spring balance (fig. 7),

in which a pointer is attached to the spring, and marks are made on a scale over which the pointer moves, to show the extent to which the spring is stretched, by weights of 1 lb., 2 lbs., &c.

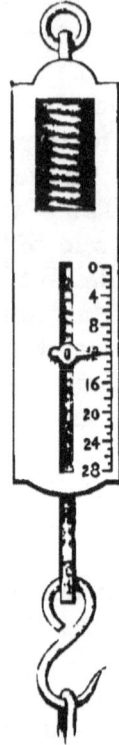

Fig. 7.*

77. Gravitation acts at all distances, but varies in intensity according to the distance between the attracting molecules; getting less very quickly when the distance is made greater, and getting greater very quickly when the distance is lessened. A force which does this is said to vary **inversely** with the distance.

78. But the above is not an exact statement of the law. In scientific work we ought not to be satisfied with knowing in a general way that the force varies when the distance varies; we should endeavour to find out precisely *how much* it varies for a given change of the distance. Sir Isaac Newton was the first to discover the simple and exact law of the variation, which will next be explained.

79. Suppose that A and B are two bodies attracting each other at a distance of 1 mile with a force equivalent to 1 grain. Then if B is removed to twice the distance—that is, 2 miles—the force of attraction is found to be $\frac{1}{4}$ of a grain. At a distance of 3 miles it is found to be only $\frac{1}{9}$ of a grain; at 4 miles, $\frac{1}{16}$ of a grain. If the distance is lessened to half a mile, the attraction becomes as great as 4 grains; and at $\frac{1}{3}$ of a mile, it is 9 grains. The result of experiments may be expressed in the following way:

Distance,	$\frac{1}{3}$ $\frac{1}{2}$	1	2	3	4	miles.
	A ● ○○	● B	○	○	○	
Force,	9 4	1	$\frac{1}{4}$	$\frac{1}{9}$	$\frac{1}{16}$	grains.

We have to examine whether there is any definite relation between the numbers denoting the distances and those denoting the amounts of attraction. Now, starting with the facts that the

* Part of the front plate has been removed to show the spiral spring inside.

square of a number is the product of the number multiplied by itself, and that the inverse or reciprocal of a number is obtained by expressing the number as a fraction (if not already one), and inverting it—that is, making the numerator denominator, and the denominator numerator (thus, $2 = \frac{2}{1}$, inverted $= \frac{1}{2}$), it is easy to see that the numbers in one of the above rows are the inverses or reciprocals of the squares of the corresponding numbers in the other row. Thus $\frac{1}{3}$ squared $= \frac{1}{9}$, inverted $= \frac{9}{1}$ or 9 : 2 squared $= 4 = \frac{4}{1}$, inverted $= \frac{1}{4}$, and so on.

80. The law, then, deduced from such experiments as the above may be stated as follows:

THE ATTRACTION OF GRAVITATION VARIES IN THE SAME PROPORTION AS THE INVERSE OF THE SQUARE OF THE DISTANCE BETWEEN THE BODIES WHICH ARE ATTRACTING EACH OTHER.

Or more shortly—

GRAVITATION VARIES INVERSELY WITH THE SQUARE OF THE DISTANCE.*

81. Thus, in order to calculate the change in the force of gravitation for any given change of distance, it is only requisite to work out the following proportion sum:

Inverse of square . Inverse of square .. Force at . Force at
of orig. distance ˙ of changed distance ˙˙ orig. distance ˙ changed distance.

82. It is clear, from what is said above, that the weight of bodies is liable to variation: for instance, things outside the earth will weigh less in proportion as they are taken farther from the earth's centre. We cannot find this out by weighing them in a pair of scales, since the pieces of metal used as weights would have their attraction altered just as much as the things which were being weighed. Some other method, such as a spring-balance, must be used; the attraction of cohesion which causes the elasticity of a spring does not vary according to the same law as gravitation.†

---

* It may be noted that this same law holds good in many other cases besides gravitation; it applies, in fact, to all phenomena which are due to an influence radiating in all directions from a centre, such as magnetic attraction, intensity of radiant heat and light, &c.

† An extremely accurate method of measuring small variations in the force of gravitation consists in observing the number of swings made in a given time by the same pendulum at different places; the greater the attractive force, the quicker the pendulum swings. A fuller account of the pendulum will be found on p. 122.

83. Anything which weighs exactly 1 lb. on the ground will, if taken to the top of a house 30 feet high, weigh $\frac{1}{80}$ of a grain less than a pound, a quantity easily measurable. If taken in a balloon to a height of 4 miles above the ground, it will weigh 14 grains less, losing, in fact, $\frac{1}{500}$ of its original weight. If it was taken to a place as far off as the moon, we can calculate what its weight would be by applying the law explained above. Thus, the distance from the earth's surface to its centre is 4000 miles (nearly); the distance from the moon to the earth's centre is 240,000 miles (nearly). These numbers are in the proportion of 1 : 60, so that the 1 lb. weight, when at the distance of the moon, will be 60 times as far from the earth's centre as it was at first. Then, from par. 81,

$$\frac{1}{1^2} : \frac{1}{60^2} :: \overset{\text{lb.}}{1} : \overset{\text{lb.}}{\frac{1}{3600}}$$

so that the body would weigh only 2.16 grains, and be 'as light as a feather.'

84. Even at different parts of the earth's surface things do not weigh the same. Anything which weighs 1 lb. at the poles is found to weigh 36 grains less at the equator: so that, for instance, we should (if a spring-balance were used) get more sugar in a pound at the equator than at the poles. There are two main reasons for this variation in weight.

(*a*) Because the earth is not quite round, but bulges out a little at the equator; its shape being, in fact, a spheroid (roughly speaking, like that of an orange), and not an exact sphere. Hence anything on the surface at the equator is 13 miles farther from the centre than it would be at the poles, and therefore the attraction of gravitation is less.

(*b*) Because anything which is revolving round a centre shows a tendency to get farther from the centre (which is called 'centrifugal tendency,' and is more fully explained on p. 51); and the quicker the body is moving, the more strongly this tendency is shown. Now, bodies at the poles, which are the extremities of the axis of rotation of the earth, are not moving relatively to this axis, while bodies on the surface of the earth at the equator are moving at the rate of 1000 miles an hour, and the centrifugal tendency due to this enormous velocity partly overcomes gravitation. If the earth turned round seventeen times faster than it actually does, the centrifugal tendency would increase so much that it would just balance the attraction of gravitation at the equator, and things on the surface there would show no weight at all.

Section 13.—Mass and Weight.

85. It is necessary to insist on the fundamental distinction between these two terms, which are often used in common language as if they meant the same thing. In weighing different things (at the same place) we notice that some are much heavier than others. Two principal reasons may be assigned for this difference in weight.

(*a*) There may be more molecules in the substance to be attracted and to attract. Thus, two cubic inches of lead weigh more than one cubic inch of lead, obviously because there are more molecules in the former than in the latter.

(*b*) Each molecule of one substance may have more of the property of gravitation (just as it may have more or less of the property of cohesion) than each molecule of the other substance. Thus a cubic inch of lead weighs more than a cubic inch of iron (although there are probably about the same number of molecules in each*), because with each molecule of lead there can be associated more of the attractive force of gravitation than with each molecule of iron. We express this by saying that there is more 'matter' in a lead-molecule than in an iron-molecule, or that its 'mass' is greater; meaning by 'matter' here simply something which can be associated with, and acted on by forces: the more there is of this, the more force can reside in it and act.

86. **Mass**, then, means strictly the *quantity of matter* in a body, while **weight** means the *amount of its attraction towards the earth's centre*. And although we commonly express the masses of things in terms of that particular result of the quantity of matter in them which we call their weight, and may truly and accurately compare the masses of two bodies by comparing their weights

---

* It is pretty certain, at any rate, that equal volumes of gases, whatever their nature, contain (when measured under the same conditions of temperature and pressure) the same number of molecules.

under the same conditions, yet the following considerations will show that the two terms are perfectly distinct.

87. The *weight* of a body varies with the place where it is, as already seen. At the centre of the earth it has no weight: at the distance of the moon it has comparatively little weight. But the *mass* of it, or the quantity of matter in it, is obviously the same, whatever may be its position.

88. The force expended in kicking a football along the ground depends upon the *mass* of the ball, and not directly upon its *weight:* the same effort would be required to set it in motion with the same speed, wherever it was in the universe. But the force expended in lifting it from the ground depends upon its weight as well as its mass.

Section 14.—Density.

89. In speaking of the 'density' of a substance, we take into account its size as well as its mass. Suppose that 2 cubic feet of air are compressed into a volume of 1 cubic foot. Then the mass of the air is, of course, in no way altered, but there is twice as much matter in the 1 cubic foot of compressed air as in 1 cubic foot of air under ordinary conditions. The compressed air is then said to have twice the 'density' of ordinary air.

90. Density, then, means the **mass of, or quantity of matter in, a given volume of a substance**. In comparing the densities of different things, some particular substance, such as water in the case of liquids and solids, is taken as the standard of comparison, and equal volumes of it and other substances have their masses compared, usually by weighing them under the same conditions. The number which expresses how much heavier or lighter a certain volume of any substance is than the *same* volume of water, is called the **specific gravity**, or (since mass is found, under the same conditions, to be proportional to weight) the **relative density** of the substance. Thus, in saying that the density of lead is $11\frac{1}{2}$, we imply that a certain volume of lead (such as a cubic inch or cubic centimetre) weighs $11\frac{1}{2}$ times as much as the same volume of water.

91. The following table shows the comparative densities of a few of the more familiar substances:

Table of Densities, or Specific Gravities, of Liquids and Solids.

Water	1·00	Glass (flint)	3·3
Platinum	21·5	Marble	2·8
Gold	19·3	Aluminium	2·6
Mercury	13·6	Porcelain	2·4
Lead	11·5	Sulphur	2·0
Silver	10·5	Boxwood	1·3
Copper	8·9	Ice	0·9
Iron	7·8	Alcohol	0·8
Diamond	3·5	Cork	0·3

92. In the case of gases, they are all (under ordinary pressures) so much less dense than water, that air is usually taken as the standard of comparison. It is preferable, however, for many reasons, to take hydrogen (the least dense of all known kinds of matter) as the standard. Fractions are thus in a great measure avoided, and (as explained more fully in the text-book on Chemistry) the comparative mass of the molecules of each substance is indicated with some certainty.

Table of Densities, or Specific Gravities, of Gases.

	Air = 1·00.	Hydrogen = 1·00.
Chlorine	2·47	35·5
Carbon Dioxide	1·53	22
('Carbonic Acid')		
Oxygen	1·10	16
Nitrogen	0·97	14
Steam	0·62	9
Hydrogen	0·07	1

CHAPTER II.

MOTION—FORCE—MOMENTUM.

Section 1.—Motion and Velocity.

93. Motion means change of place. When anything which has been observed to be in one place, is found after an interval of time to be in another place, we say that it has 'moved.' We find out, for instance, whether a clock is going by noting whether the hands point, as time goes on, to different figures on the dial. We ascertain whether a distant ship is sailing on, or lying at anchor, by observing whether or not it is seen at successive intervals on different points of the horizon, or in different positions with regard to other ships. But here there often arises a considerable difficulty. How are we to know whether these ships are not themselves moving, while the one we are watching is really motionless?

94. When two trains are standing at a station, and one of them begins to move, it is at first not easy for a passenger to tell with certainty whether it is the train in which he is, or the other train, which is in motion, without a reference to something which is considered most likely to be fixed, such as the walls of the station. But these walls are undoubtedly themselves in rapid motion with the surface of the earth on which they stand; only we do not perceive their motion because they are moving in every respect similarly to the earth's surface. Moreover, the earth itself is all the time in still swifter motion round the sun, and the sun with all the planets is moving through space, we know not whither. Scientific investigations point to the fact that nothing, not even a single molecule of the hardest solid, is absolutely at rest. In short, all that we can distinguish and judge of is *relative motion*—that is, whether a body is moving at a different rate, or in a different direction to another body with which we compare it. If a boat sails against a stream exactly as fast as the stream flows, it is at rest relatively to the bottom

and banks, but in motion as regards the water. *Absolute motion* means change of place with regard to space itself. But we have no means of marking a fixed point in space, and therefore we can never observe such a motion.

95. **Velocity** means **rate of motion.** It is generally expressed by stating how far the body would move in a certain time, such as one second, if the rate of motion continued uniform. Thus, in saying that a cannon-ball moves with a velocity of 1400 feet per second, we mean that if it went on at the same rate, it would at the end of one second be 1400 feet from the place where it was at the beginning of the second. In this sense a train is said, with perfect correctness, to be travelling with a velocity of 60 miles an hour, although very few trains ever cover 60 miles in that space of time. The velocity is *uniform*, when equal spaces are always passed over in equal times; it is *accelerated*, when gradually increased, and *retarded*, when gradually diminished. If the increase or diminution is equal in equal times, the motion is said to be *uniformly accelerated* or *uniformly retarded*.

Section 2.—Force.

96. **Matter cannot set itself in motion.** A ball placed on a level table remains where it is put, and will remain there so long as the conditions are unaltered. Some power or influence must act on it to make it move; and any power which does this is called a 'force.' It is equally true that (as will be explained more fully in Chapter III.), when the ball is once for all set in motion, it will not stop or turn aside from a straight course unless some force is applied.

97. Force, then, may be defined as **that which produces motion, or changes motion, or destroys motion.** No one has ever seen forces; they have none of the properties of ordinary matter; in fact, they are not forms of matter at all, they are influences which give life, as it were, to the dead materials of the universe. We only recognise them by their effects. When we observe a body moving, we know that some force must have acted on it; if it increases its speed, we know that some force must be acting on it still; if it swerves aside or stops, we know that another force has been at work.

40 ELEMENTARY DYNAMICS.

98. The following will serve as examples of the more commonly occurring forces:

(*a*) **Gravitation**: which makes a stone fall; keeps most ordinary clocks going; moves a train down an incline; changes the motion of the earth from a straight line to a curve round the sun.

(*b*) **Cohesion**: which is acting in an elastic spring, such as that which keeps a watch going; and when a falling stone touches any hard surface, destroys the motion which gravitation has caused.

(*c*) **Muscular action**: which enables us to raise a weight, move from place to place, hit or throw a cricket-ball.

99. In considering the action of forces, three things have to be taken into account: (1) the **point** at which the force is applied;* (2) its **direction**—that is, the line in which it tends to make the body move; (3) its **magnitude**—that is, the amount of it as determined by the effect it produces. Both the direction and the magnitude of a force can be conveniently and accurately represented by drawing a line of a definite length. The direction of the line will denote, of course, the direction in which the force acts, and the length of the line, adjusted to any definite scale such as inches or centimetres, may indicate the magnitude of the force.

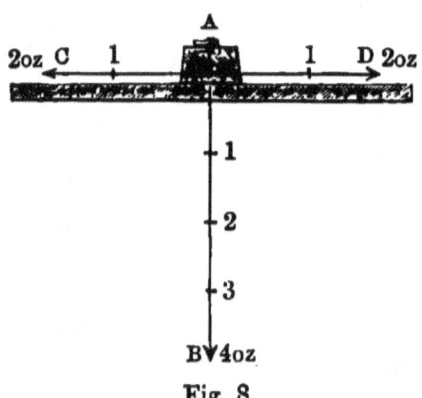

Fig. 8.

100. Suppose, for instance, that a weight of 4 oz. is resting on a table, and is pulled in opposite directions by two forces, each equivalent to 2 oz. These conditions can be represented by the following diagram, fig. 8, in which A is the body; AB, 4 units long (on any convenient scale, such as inches or centimetres), will denote the magnitude and direction

---

* As will be seen later on, p. 110, however large or irregular in shape a body may be, a single point can always be found in it (called the 'centre of inertia'), at which a force may be considered to be applied, and will produce the same effect as if it acted on every separate molecule of the mass.

of the force of gravitation ; AC and AD, each 2 units long on the same scale, will represent the forces pulling it to the right and left respectively.

101. Equilibrium of Forces.—The case represented in the above diagram affords a good illustration of the fact that a force does not necessarily actually produce motion. The weight A is really acted on by four forces : (1) gravitation, pulling it downward ; (2) the cohesion of the molecules of the table, which holds them together against the pressure of the weight, and supplies a force which just counteracts the force of gravitation ; (3) the force AC ; (4) the force AD. The last two, being equal in magnitude and opposite in direction, obviously just counteract each other, like the first two ; and so the weight A does not move at all. When forces balance each other in this way, so that the body acted on does not move, they are said to be 'in **equilibrium.'**

Section 3.—Momentum.

102. A moving body clearly has force associated with it. It can set other things in motion. A cricket-ball can knock down the wicket ; a cannon-ball, a train, an iceberg, will overthrow obstacles which are so unfortunate as to come in their way. Even particles so light as those of air may have force enough to produce great effects, as proved by the destructive power of hurricanes.

103. **Momentum is the term used to express the force with which anything is moving.** It is found to be proportional to (a) the **velocity,** (b) the **mass** of the moving body. The heavier a thing is, and the quicker it is moving, the greater is the momentum which it has. The amount of momentum can be conveniently expressed by the number obtained by multiplying the mass of a body (stated in pounds, grammes, &c.) by its velocity in feet or centimetres per second. The product of these numbers is called the 'momentum' of the body. For instance, if a cannonball weighing 9 lbs. is moving with a velocity of 500 feet per second, its momentum is said to be ($9 \times 500 =$) **4500** (in lbs. ft. sec.). If another ball weighing 3 lbs. is moving 1500 feet per second, its momentum is ($3 \times 1500 =$) **4500.**

104. We observe that the momenta of the two balls are equal,

although one is so much lighter than the other. In fact, in order that a body may move with great force—that is, have a great momentum—it is sufficient that *either* its mass *or* its velocity should be great. Thus a rifle-ball, though very light, has a high momentum because its velocity is so great. Hailstones, though very small, do much damage because they reach the earth with great velocity. An iceberg, though it moves very slowly, has great momentum because its mass is enormous, so that it will slowly but surely crush a ship.

Section 4.—Measurement of Forces.

105. If the power of a locomotive engine had to be found, we might estimate it either (*a*) by seeing how many horses pulling against it would just keep it from moving, or (*b*) by seeing with what velocity it would move a train of known weight. Thus we might compare it with other engines or motive powers.

106. Speaking generally, there are two principal ways of finding the magnitude of a force.

(*a*) We may find out how much of some more easily measurable force is required to balance it, so as to get equilibrium.

(*b*) We may find out how much momentum it produces in a certain time, such as 1 second.

For example, the magnitude of gravitation may be measured:

(*a*) By observing how far a certain mass, such as 1 lb., when acted on by it, would stretch a spring; thus balancing gravitation against cohesion.

(*b*) By allowing it to act on a certain mass, such as 1 lb., for 1 second, and observing what velocity it produces in the body; since from these data the momentum can be calculated, as already explained.

107. The subject of the measurement of forces will be more fully considered in the next chapter. It is mentioned here in order to make clear the distinction between the two branches into which Dynamics is divided—namely, Statics and Kinetics. These differ mainly in the methods employed in them for the measurement of forces.

In **Statics** (στατικὸς, *that which makes to stop*), the magnitude of a force is measured by the first of the two methods described above—that is, by balancing it against another force, so that no motion is produced in the body acted on.

In **Kinetics** ($\kappa\acute{\iota}\nu\eta\sigma\iota\varsigma$, *movement*), the magnitude of a force is measured by the second method—namely, by observing what momentum it produces.

108. In what follows, the action of forces will be treated mainly on the principles of kinetics. It is obviously best to observe the direct effect of a force as shown by the motion it produces, instead of complicating matters by introducing other, and possibly less understood, agencies to balance it.

APPENDIX.

Problems on Momentum.

In questions relating to the momentum of bodies, there are three quantities to be taken account of—

    1. **Mass.**   2. **Velocity.**   3. **Momentum.**

If we know any two of these three quantities, a very simple arithmetical process will enable us to find the third.

1. When mass and velocity are known. Then, as above explained, mass × velocity = momentum.

EXAMPLE.—A bird weighing 3 lbs. is observed to be flying at the rate of 50 feet per second. Hence its momentum will be,
$$3 \times 50 = 150.$$

2. When momentum and mass are known. Then it may be proved* that $\dfrac{\text{momentum}}{\text{mass}}$ = velocity.

EXAMPLE.—A cannon-ball weighing 12 lbs. has a momentum of 10,800: what must be its velocity?
$$\frac{10,800}{12} = 900 \text{ feet per second.}$$

3. When momentum and velocity are known. Then $\dfrac{\text{momentum}}{\text{velocity}}$ = mass.

---

* Suppose a, b, and c are three quantities so related that $a \times b = c$. Then to find b when a and c are known, divide both sides of the equation by a.
$$\frac{ab}{a} = \frac{c}{a}. \quad \text{That is, cancelling } a \text{ on left side, } b = \frac{c}{a}.$$
Similarly, to find a, divide both sides by b.
$$\frac{ab}{b} = \frac{c}{b}. \quad \text{That is, } a = \frac{c}{b}.$$

EXAMPLE.—A boat which is being rowed at the rate of 20 feet per second has a momentum of 36,000. Then its weight must be
$$\frac{36,000}{20} = 1800 \text{ lbs.}$$

CHAPTER III.

LAWS OF MOTION.

109. The chief facts observed respecting the movements of bodies have been summed up in the form of a few general propositions, which were first put into shape by Sir Isaac Newton under the name of laws of motion. They may be considered as statements of universal rules by which the action of forces on matter appears to be guided. We shall first give them nearly in the form in which they were laid down by Sir Isaac Newton himself, and then proceed to a fuller explanation of each.

Law I.—**A body, if it is at rest, will continue at rest; and if it is in motion, will continue in motion in a straight line with uniform velocity, unless some force acts on it.**

This law teaches us how we can recognise the existence of a force—namely, by observing its effect in changing the state of rest or motion of a body.

Law II.—**The momentum produced by a force is exactly proportional to the magnitude of the force: and when several forces act on a body, each produces motion in its own direction, just as if it was the only force acting.**

From this law we learn (1) how the magnitude of a force may be accurately measured—namely, by observing how much momentum it produces; (2) how we can estimate the joint effect of several forces acting all at once upon a body; the direction, for instance, a football will take when kicked by two players simultaneously.

Law III.—**The action of a force is always accompanied by a reaction of the body to which it is applied. This reaction is equal in magnitude, but opposite in direction to the original force.**

In this law we consider the effect of the communication of force, not merely on the body to which it is imparted, but also on the body which imparts it.

SECTION 1.—THE FIRST LAW OF MOTION.

A body, if it is at rest, will continue at rest; and if it is in motion, will continue in motion in a straight line with uniform velocity, unless some force acts on it.

110. This law is little else than a full definition of the property of matter which is called 'Inertia' (Lat. *inertia*, inactivity)—namely, the inability of a body to change of its own accord its state of rest or of movement (alluded to already in par. 96, p. 39). It will be convenient to divide the law into three distinct statements, and examine each of them separately.

(A) **Matter cannot set itself in motion.**

111. Even the smallest particle of dust will remain passively where it has settled on a shelf or carpet until a brush or a breeze (like a member of the police 'force') makes it 'move on.' A heavy train requires a great force to start it; in fact, the inertia, or passive resistance to change, of a body is found to be exactly proportional to its mass.

112. If there are several things resting close together or loosely joined, and a force is applied to one of them, that one alone will move, and break away from the rest, which will remain still because of their inertia. A simple experiment will illustrate this statement. Let a card be balanced upon the tip of the finger, and a shilling (or other bit of metal about the same in size) be laid upon it (fig. 9). Let the card then be smartly struck or filliped away;

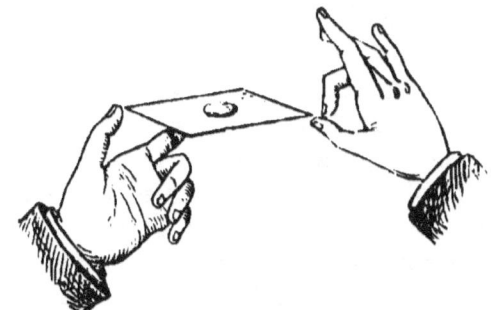

Fig. 9.

it will fly from beneath the coin, leaving the latter supported on the finger. The inertia of the metal causes it to retain its place; while the card, to which alone force was applied, passes from beneath it. For the same reason, when a horse starts unexpectedly, or bolts, the rider may lose his seat, remaining where he was, while the horse shoots on. When a train or a boat starts with a jerk, passengers who happen to be standing up are liable to be 'thrown down' (as we incorrectly say), owing to their inability to take up at once the motion of the surface on which they are standing. So also the difficulty of carrying along a glass full of water without spilling any, arises from the inertia of the particles of water keeping them in their places when the glass begins to move, or changes the direction or rate of its movement from unsteadiness of the hand which holds it, or irregularity of the pace in walking.

113. The process of beating a carpet, or dusting a book, rests on the same principle as the experiment with the shilling and the card. The carpet being struck, is suddenly put in motion, while the particles of dust remain where they were, their inertia being sufficient to overcome the slight force with which they adhere to the surface of the carpet. When a dusty book is struck against a table, the book and the dust are first brought into rapid motion together, and the book being then arrested by the table, the dust continues in motion by its inertia, and is thus detached. Skaters are often able to glide over dangerously thin ice without its breaking, if they move quickly; because the pressure is taken off each successive particle of the ice before there is time to overcome its inertia and break it away from the rest. Many a train has escaped a serious accident owing to the high speed at which it has passed over a loose rail or an unsafe bridge; the inertia of the rail, &c., keeping them in place while the train shoots over them. The common feat of breaking a stick resting on two wine-glasses depends on the suddenness of the blow; the stick is broken before the pressure upon the glass supports has had time to overcome the inertia of their molecules and beat them down. A candle fired from a gun will make a clear hole through a board half an inch thick; the inertia of the particles of tallow keeping them nearly in their places while the wood is penetrated.

(B) **Matter cannot stop itself when moving.**

114. That a body at rest will continue at rest, unless acted on by something, seems so obvious that no one perhaps ever thought of asserting the contrary. Why do we not as readily assent to the statement that a body, once in motion, will never stop unless something stops it? The reason is, that in all ordinary cases we observe that things moving, such as a cannon-ball, a spinning top, *do* soon come to a standstill. But, in fact, there are forces acting on these to lessen, and finally destroy their motion; such as friction and inertia of the particles of air which are flung aside by the moving body. A ball rolled along rough ground soon stops; on a smooth pavement it continues longer in motion; and on smooth ice, longer still. A common top continues to spin for a greater length of time than it usually does, when placed in a space from which the air has been extracted by an air-pump. Thus we learn that, as the obstructions to its motion are lessened or removed, a body will go on moving longer and longer; and we may infer that if *all* obstructions could be removed, the motion would go on for ever.

115. We cannot realise such conditions in our experiments; but we have in the earth and the other planets and heavenly bodies, excellent examples of free, unobstructed motion, and here the most accurate observations have failed to detect any sensible slackening of speed.* The length of the day of 24 hours (which, of course, depends upon the rotation of the earth on its axis) has probably not varied one-tenth of a second since the earliest astronomical observations were made about 2000 years ago. Scientific reasoning, then, leads us to the conclusion that motion, if unobstructed, no more requires to be kept up by the continued action of a force than rest, and that matter retains a state of motion no less easily than a state of rest.

116. Many illustrations can be given of the results and applications of the inertia of bodies which are moving. In jumping, it is found of great advantage to take a short run before the

---

* It is true that in the case of one small comet a perceptible retardation of motion has been observed; but the amount is no greater than can be fairly attributed to the resistance of the small amount of matter which undoubtedly exists throughout all space, and which may in the course of millions of years produce a measurable effect on the motions of the earth and planets.

actual jump, because the forward motion thus gained continues after the feet leave the ground, and thus not only is the body carried farther, as in the 'long jump,' but also in the 'high jump' the muscles have only the work of raising the body to the height of the bar, the forward motion necessary to clear it being given by the inertia due to the run. Riders in a circus, when jumping through hoops from the back of a galloping horse, soon learn that they must spring *upward* only, and not forward, if they wish to alight on the horse's back after passing through the hoop. A man jumping from a moving carriage or train will certainly fall prostrate on the ground, if he leaps down as if he were descending from a carriage which is standing still; for when he makes the attempt, his body has the same motion as the carriage, and when his feet touch the ground, their motion is arrested while the velocity of the upper part of the body continues; and thus he finds himself thrown down.

117. **Coursing, or hare-hunting, affords a striking illustration of inertia.** In that field-sport, the hare seems to possess an instinctive consciousness of the existence of this law of motion. When pursued by the greyhound, it does not run in a straight line to the cover; but in a zigzag one. It *doubles*—that is, suddenly changes the direction of its course, and turns back at an acute angle with the direction in which it had been running. The greyhound being unprepared to make the turn, and therefore unable to resist the tendency to persevere in the rapid motion which it has acquired, is impelled a considerable distance forward before it can check its speed and return to the pursuit. But, in the meantime, the hare has been enabled to shoot far ahead in the other direction; and although a hare is much less fleet than a greyhound, by this scientific manœuvring it often escapes its pursuer. Those who have witnessed horse-racing may have observed that the horses shoot far past the winning-post before their speed can be arrested. This is also owing to the inertia of their bodies.

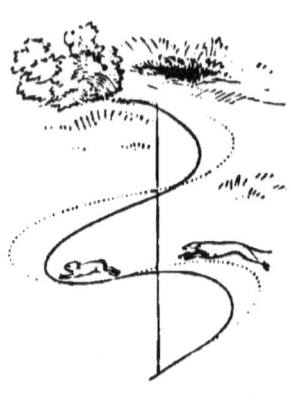

Fig. 10.

118. When several bodies are moving close together or loosely joined, and *one* of them is stopped by a force, the others still go on moving because of their inertia. For instance, in throwing a cricket-ball, or a stone, the hand moves with the ball at first, but is checked at the proper moment, and the ball goes on moving with the same speed, and in the same direction, as the hand was moving at the moment when it let go the ball. The whole art of taking a good shot at the wicket, or other object, depends on letting go the ball or stone precisely at the moment when it and the hand are moving in the direction and with the speed required to hit the object.

119. When a horse suddenly stops, as in refusing a jump, the rider has a tendency to go on moving, and thus he may be, in the correct sense of the word, 'thrown' from his seat over the head of the horse. Passengers in a train which comes into collision with another train, or any such obstacle, continue moving forward with the same speed as the carriage was moving before it was checked by the collision, and are thus thrown violently against the side of the carriage and 'severely shaken.'

(C) **A single force can only produce motion in a straight line.**

120. For example, a stone, when acted on by gravitation alone, falls in a straight line towards the earth's centre : a billiard ball, when struck, moves in a straight line over a level table. Hence, whenever we observe a moving body deviate from a straight line, we may be sure that some force must be acting on it to make it do so. A cannon-ball, as soon as it leaves the mouth of the gun, does not continue to move straight onward, but deviates in a curve downwards, because gravitation is acting freely upon it, and changes the direction of its original motion.

121. If a falling ball has a string attached to it, which is tied to a fixed point on one side, it will move in a curve, because the cohesion of the string supplies a force which makes it bend more and more from the straight line in which gravitation alone would make it move. If the end of the string is held in the hand, and the ball is whirled round, there are two forces acting on it, namely—(1) the force applied by the hand, which moves it onward against the resistance of the air ; (2) a force also applied by the hand, and acting through the string, which keeps

it from moving straight on as it naturally would do, and pulls it inward so as to keep it at a fixed distance from the centre round which it is whirled.

122. While it is moving in this circle, it shows a tendency to get farther from the centre, which is called **centrifugal tendency** (Lat. *centrum*, a centre, and *fugio*, I fly). This is simply a consequence of the inertia of the ball. Let A, fig. 11, represent the ball. When set in motion, it would naturally, as above stated, go on in the straight line, AB; force, therefore, has to be exerted through the string, AC, in order to pull it away from the straight line, and owing to its inertia there is resistance to this force. Thus centrifugal tendency is not a real force itself, as it was formerly considered to be, urging the body directly away from the centre.

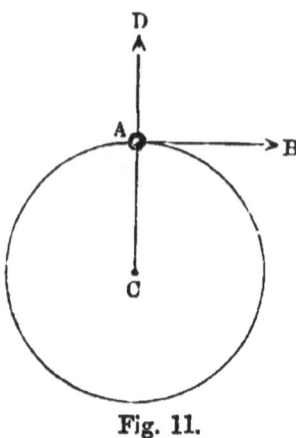

Fig. 11.

123. That it is not so is sufficiently proved by observing the result of letting go, or cutting, the string at the moment the ball reaches the point A. If any real centrifugal *force* was being exerted, then (since a force causes motion in its own direction) the ball would move in the direction AD. But it does not do so; it simply goes on in the direction in which it was moving at the moment it was set free, namely, in the line AB.

124. The same is true at whatever point in the circle the ball is released. Thus, if released at E, fig. 12, it takes the direction EF; if at G, the direction GH, and so on. Now, at any point in a circle, the direction of the curve is that of a straight line drawn through the point at right angles to the radius. Such a straight line is called a 'tangent,' and hence we can express generally the direction which the ball takes when set free from the constraining force, by saying that it flies off at a 'tangent.'

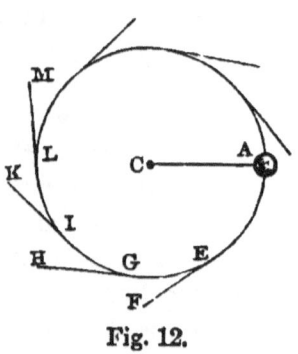

Fig. 12.

Section 2.—Laws of Centrifugal Tendency.

[For illustrating the facts and laws of centrifugal tendency, a so-called 'whirling table' (fig. 13) is extremely convenient. It consists

Fig. 13.

of a firm base-board, near one end of which is fitted an upright spindle carrying a small pulley. On the same board a large grooved wheel is fitted, and connected by a cord with the small pulley, so that by turning the wheel the vertical spindle may be made to rotate very quickly. This spindle has a screw nose at the top, to which various pieces of apparatus can be fitted.]

125. The centrifugal tendency of a body moving in a circle varies in amount according to the following laws:

I. **It increases with the mass of the body.**

A ball weighing 2 lbs. resists the bending from its straight course with twice as much force as a ball weighing 1 lb., under the same conditions of velocity, &c. For the inertia of a body varies with the mass (par. 111), and centrifugal tendency is, as above explained, a consequence of inertia.

II. **It varies (for a given velocity) inversely with the radius of the circle in which the body moves**; getting less in proportion as the radius is greater, and greater as the radius is less.

126. For the smaller the size of the circle in which the body is compelled to move, the sharper is the curve described by it, and hence the greater is the distance through which it has to be dragged out of its straight course in a given time. Thus, if ACX, fig. 14, is a circle of 2 feet radius, and AB is the distance through which the body, A, would move in 1 second, if it went on in a straight line, then it has to be dragged

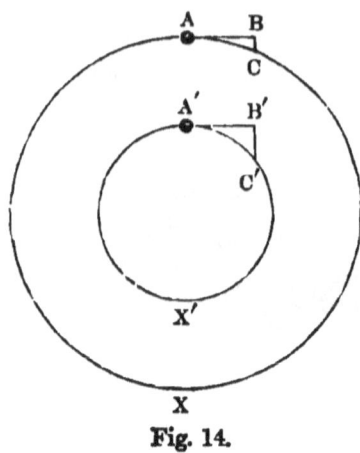

Fig. 14.

through the distance BC in 1 second in order to keep it in the circumference of the circle. And if A'C'X' represents another circle with a radius of only 1 foot, it is clear that a body A' having the same mass and the same velocity, will have to be dragged through the distance B'C' in 1 second. Now B'C' can easily be proved (for small arcs) to be twice BC; thus the inertia of A' has to be overcome through twice as great a distance as in the case of A, so that A' shows twice as much centrifugal tendency.

III. It increases with the square of the velocity.

127. Thus, a body moving round a centre with a velocity of 1 foot per second, shows a certain amount of centrifugal tendency. If its velocity in the same circle is increased to 2 feet per second, it shows (not twice, but) 4 times, that is, 2×2 (or 2^2) times, as much centrifugal tendency. The reason will be plain if we consider that the body, when it is travelling twice as fast as it originally was, (1) has to be dragged out of its straight course through twice the distance in a given time;* (2) has to be moved through this double distance at twice the rate, in order to keep it in the circle. Thus, altogether 2×2 times the force has to be used; and the centrifugal tendency is measured by the force required to overcome it.

Similarly, if the velocity of the body is increased to 3 feet per second, the centrifugal tendency becomes 9 times—that is, 3×3 times, its original amount.

128. If a solid body is pierced by a straight rod, and made to turn on it as on an axis (as, for example, a wheel or a grind-

---

* This will be plain by reference to fig. 12, p. 50. Suppose that, to begin with, the body has such a speed that it travels in one second from E to G, in the circle, and therefore has to be deflected from F to G in that time. Then, if its speed is doubled, it will reach I in 1 second, and so will have to be deflected from H to I, as well as from F to G, in the time. Hence, it will undergo two deflections instead of one only—that is, will be deflected through twice the distance in 1 second.

stone), every particle of the body describes a circle round this axis. All these circles are described in the same time; and the larger they are, the quicker the particle must move in order to complete the circle in the time. In fact, the velocity increases in the same proportion as the radius of the circle, so that particles which are 2 feet from the axis, move twice as fast as those which are 1 foot from the axis. Hence, it is clear that the centrifugal tendency of the outer particles will be much greater than that of the particles near the axis; although the increased centrifugal tendency due to increase of velocity (Law III.), is partly compensated by the decrease caused by the greater size of the circle described (Law II.). Thus, the fourth law of centrifugal tendency may be stated as follows:

IV. **When a number of particles describe circles of different sizes in the same time, the centrifugal tendency of each is in direct proportion to the radius of the circle described.**

We proceed in the next place to give some illustrations and practical applications of centrifugal tendency.

129. In slinging a stone, the latter is whirled in the sling round the hand as a centre, until a great velocity, and therefore, a great centrifugal tendency, is attained, and it is let go at the moment when it has reached a point in the circle, the tangent to which is in the direction of the object aimed at. The same is, of course, true of the athletic sport of 'throwing the hammer'; the long handle of the hammer serving the purpose of a sling. The ordinary process of throwing a stone and bowling a cricket-ball is of much the same nature, but the hand then only describes a portion of a circle of which the shoulder is the centre. In all such cases, the main difficulty is to judge correctly the proper moment at which the ball or the stone is to be set free to follow the direction in which its inertia will keep it moving.

130. In rapidly-moving parts of machinery there is often great danger of breakage, owing to the high centrifugal tendency of those portions which are at a great distance from the axis of rotation. Thus, large fly-wheels have been known to break to pieces when the engine has from any cause begun to move faster than usual. Similarly, the massive grindstones used in cutlery

works sometimes break up without any warning, and the flying fragments cause great damage owing to their mass and velocity, like stones from an immense sling.*

131. Wet mops are easily and quickly dried by twirling them rapidly round on their handles as axes of rotation; the particles of water travel to the extremities of the woollen strands, their centrifugal tendency increasing as they get farther from the centre (Law IV.), and then they fly off in well-marked tangent lines. Mud is thrown off from a quickly-moving carriage wheel in a similar way.

132. In sugar manufactories, the crystallised sugar is separated from the liquid syrup by placing the whole in a cylindrical vessel, the sides of which are perforated with small holes like a sieve. This is turned quickly round at a rate of 1500 or 2000 revolutions a minute, and the liquid portions fly out through the holes into a surrounding vessel, leaving the sugar nearly dry. Clothes are dried in many laundries in a very similar machine called a 'centrifugal extractor.'

Fig. 15.

[This can be illustrated by attaching to the upright spindle of the whirling table a large glass cup with rim turned inward (shaped like the bowls in which goldfish are kept), placing in this a little water coloured with ink or indigo, and making it rotate quickly. The water spreads outwards, and, as the velocity of rotation increases, leaves the bottom of the glass and forms a broad coloured band at the widest part of the cup (fig. 15), getting as far from the axis of rotation as it can.]

133. Centrifugal tendency is also usefully employed in the manufacture of 'crown' glass, or window glass. A lump of melted glass is attached to the end of an iron tube, and blown into a hollow globe (*a*, fig. 16). This is, while still soft, opened out into a cup, *b*; and this cup is held in front of a furnace, and rapidly twirled round on the iron tube as an axis. The edges of the cup soon widen out owing to centrifugal tendency, assuming

* It is interesting to notice that the very same agency, centrifugal tendency, is employed in an apparatus invented by Watt, the great engineer, for enabling the engine to regulate its own speed, and thus to prevent or render unlikely such accidents as those mentioned above. A description of this 'centrifugal governor' will be found in any treatise on the steam-engine.

the shape *c*; and finally the whole flashes out into a thin, uniform, flat sheet, *d*.

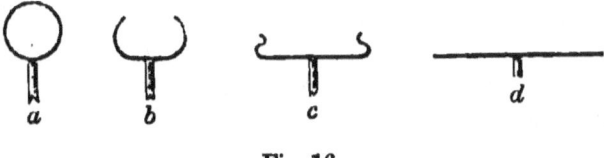

Fig. 16.

134. In equestrian performances in a circus, both rider and horse incline their bodies inwards to just such an extent that the tendency to fall inwards, due to gravitation, counteracts their centrifugal tendency; which would, if they went along upright, make it impossible for them to keep in the circle. In running round a corner, and in describing a sharp curve in skating, the same thing is done, and for a similar reason. When a curve has to be made on a railway, the rail on the outside of the curve is always raised a little above the level of the inner rail, so as to tilt the train inwards, and thus lessen the risk of its running off the rails from its tendency to persevere in a straight course.

135. We may also trace the influence of centrifugal tendency on a very large scale in the shape and motions of the bodies which make up the solar system. The earth rotates, as if on a spindle or axis the extremities of which are at the N. and S. poles, once in 24 hours. Now, since its circumference is approximately 24,000 miles, the parts of its surface at the equator must move through about 24,000 miles a day, or 1000 miles an hour, while the surface in the latitude of England has a much less rapid motion, about 640 miles an hour, and this velocity becomes less and less as the poles are approached. It follows from this that the centrifugal tendency of the particles which compose the earth must be much greater near the equator than near the poles; a fact which has two important results.

(1) There is no reason to doubt that the earth was at one time a large drop of liquid, and if it had been at rest its shape would (as explained in par. 17 *b*, p. 10) have been exactly spherical. But owing to its quick rotation, the parts of it near the equator spread outwards through their great centrifugal tendency; thus

the whole mass became spheroidal in shape, like an orange; and when it became solid it kept this shape. Hence it is that the diameter of the earth is 26 miles greater at the equator than at the poles. The planet Jupiter rotates more than twice as quickly as the earth, and it is found, as we should expect, to bulge out at the equator even more than our earth, so that it appears distinctly oval in a telescope.

[The influence of centrifugal tendency in causing this change of shape may be illustrated by rotating a large india-rubber ball (5 in., or more, in diameter) on a vertical axis attached to the spindle of the whirling table. The ball should be attached to this axis at the top only, the lower hole through which the axis passes being large enough to admit of free motion on the axis as the equatorial parts of the ball spread out. Three or four cuts in the india-rubber should be made across the equator in the direction of the meridians on a globe, reaching to about 30° from each pole: these will increase the flexibility of the india-rubber. If the ball is rotated at a moderate speed, it will assume a spheroidal shape.]

(2) All bodies on the surface of the earth are, of course, being whirled round with it, and consequently show a tendency to fly off from the surface, which partly counteracts the force of gravitation: in other words, lessens their weight (as has been already mentioned in par. 84 b, p. 34). It can be calculated from the laws above explained how much the weight of a body at the equator is, owing to its centrifugal tendency, less than what it would be if the earth was still; and it is found that a mass weighing 1 lb. at the poles weighs 24 grs. less than a pound at the equator—loses, in fact, $\frac{1}{289}$ of its weight—owing to centrifugal tendency alone. Further, it can be shown that if the earth were to rotate seventeen times faster than it does at present, the centrifugal tendency at the equator would be so greatly increased as to balance the whole force of gravitation; and a very small further increase of velocity would cause bodies to leave the surface of the earth altogether.

136. The earth is moving in its orbit round the sun with a velocity of 1080 miles a minute, or nearly 65,000 miles an hour: and the centrifugal tendency due to this enormous speed just balances the sun's force of gravitation, and maintains the earth at a definite distance from the sun. If its

onward velocity were to cease, it would fall straight upon the sun. If its velocity were to be increased about one-half, the increased centrifugal tendency would overcome the sun's attraction altogether, and the earth would get farther and farther from the sun, and never come near it again. Each of the planets and their satellites, every comet, and each component of a 'double star,' is found to be moving in just such a path as enables its centrifugal tendency to balance the force of gravitation to which it is subjected.

Section 3.—Friction.

137. It has been already stated that, although there is no doubt of the truth of the first Law of Motion, we cannot prove by experiment that moving bodies, if left to themselves, go on for ever with unaltered speed; and friction was mentioned as one great cause of this failure. We find, in fact, that whenever two surfaces are moving in contact with each other, their motion is resisted, each 'putting the drag,' as it were, on the other. This resistance to the motion of surfaces which are in contact is called '**Friction**,' and is a good example of the action of forces in checking, instead of causing motion.

138. Friction is due mainly to two causes:

(1) No surface can ever be made perfectly smooth; little inequalities are visible through a microscope in even the hardest and most carefully polished surface; and so the rough projecting parts of one surface catch against the rough parts of the other (like a couple of files laid one on the other) and hinder it in moving along.

(2) There is always some adhesion or cohesion between the molecules of the surfaces when they are brought pretty close together (par. 34, p. 16), and careful smoothing and fitting only tends to increase this, since it brings more molecules within range of each other's attraction.

Laws of Friction.

139. To investigate these it is generally most convenient to use a 'statical' method (par. 107, p. 42)—that is, to balance friction against some easily measurable force, and see how much of the latter is required for this purpose, or rather to keep the

surfaces just moving in spite of their friction. Gravitation is the best force to use, and a very simple apparatus, shown in fig. 17, will serve to illustrate these laws. It consists of a strip of well-seasoned, straight-grained oak, about 2 feet long and 5 inches broad, supported on a stand, or placed on a table so that one end projects over the edge of the table. One surface of the strip should be planed or scraped as flat and smooth as possible.* At one end of the block a pulley is attached, with a cord passing over it, to one end of which blocks of various shapes and materials may be connected, while from the other end may be hung weights or a scale-pan in which weights may be put.

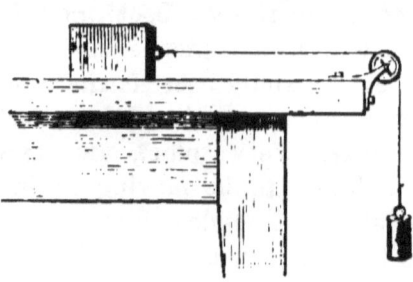

Fig. 17.

Law I.—**The friction between two surfaces is greater when they are resting in contact than when they are moving in contact with one another.**

140. To show this, a block of oak about 4 in. square × 2 in. thick is placed on the board; and weights are hung from the cord, until the amount required to set the block in motion along the board is found. It will be noticed that the block, when once started, begins to move very quickly, and that if contact between it and the board is disturbed by a slight lateral push, or even by tapping the board with the finger, a decidedly less weight is required to keep it moving steadily and slowly along the board. Hence, in subsequent experiments, the block should always be started by lightly tapping the board, in order to obtain the true moving friction.

Law II.—**Friction does not vary much with the velocity with which the surfaces are moving.**

141. There is about the same resistance to motion between a

---

* No glass-paper should be used in smoothing it, since the particles of glass get imbedded in the wood: and of course no varnish, polish, or oil should be applied.

carriage wheel and its axle, or between a sledge and the ground, or between a skate and the ice, whether the motion be fast or slow. It was formerly thought that friction was quite independent of the velocity, but recent experiments have shown that, when bearings are well lubricated, there is, fortunately for engineers, decidedly less friction in proportion at high speeds than at low ones.

Law III.—**Friction varies with the material of the surfaces, even when they are equally smooth and equally pressed together.**

142. Thus there is more friction between two pieces of wood than between two pieces of metal under similar conditions, and still more friction between wood and metal. This may easily be illustrated by experiments with the apparatus already described, and a table showing the amount of friction between different substances is given on p. 61. We learn from such experiments that wood is one of the best materials for brake-blocks, and one of the worst for bearings of axles or runners for sliding seats in boats.

Law IV.—**Friction varies directly with the pressure between the surfaces.**

143. Twice the pressure causes twice the friction; three times the pressure, three times the friction, and so on. This may be illustrated by arranging a block of wood on the board, as in the previous experiments, noting the weight required to keep it just gently moving, and then putting on it another block of the same weight. There must then, of course, be twice the original pressure between the lower surface of the block and the board; and it will be found that twice as much weight will now be required to keep the block moving. A third block may then be placed on the other two, and the resulting friction observed in like manner. Hence, the heavier an engine is, the greater is the hold which the driving-wheels have on the rail; the tighter a rope or a bat is gripped, the less likely it is to slip through the hand.

Law V.—**Friction does not vary with the size of the surfaces when the total pressure between them is unaltered.**

144. At first sight we should hardly expect this to be true; it

would seem, for instance, that a sledge must go more heavily on broad runners than on narrow ones. An experiment to test the correctness of the law may be made as follows. A wooden block, 4 inches square and 2 inches thick, has a deep broad groove cut out of one side so as to give it the section shown in fig. 18. The portions C, C, left on each side of the groove may be ¼ in. broad. Thus we can place three different-sized surfaces on the board—namely, A, the area of which is, of course, (4 in. × 4 in. =) 16 square inches; B, having an area of (4 in. × 2 in. =) 8 sq. inches; or C, C, having each an area of (¼ in. × 4 in. =) 1 sq. in., or altogether 2 sq. inches; the total pressure (which is, of course, the weight of the block) being in all three cases the same. The amount of friction between the block and the board may be determined in the usual way, and it will be found to be practically the same whether the block is resting upon A, or upon B, or upon C, C.

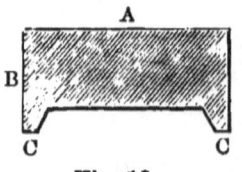

Fig. 18.

145. The reason will be plain, if we consider (1) that friction varies directly with the pressure (that is, increases and decreases in exact proportion as the pressure increases and decreases); (2) that when the surface is large the pressure is distributed over many points, and so there is not much of it on each point, while, when the surface is small (the total pressure remaining unaltered), the whole pressure is concentrated on few points, and therefore there is more of it between each point of the surfaces in contact. Suppose, for instance, that the block weighs 1 lb.; then, when it rests on A (16 sq. in.), the pressure on each sq. in. of the surface will be $\frac{1}{16}$ lb., or 1 oz.; when it rests on B (8 sq. in.), all the pressure is collected on *half* the surface, and therefore there will be twice as much, or 2 oz., on each sq. inch. So that the advantage apparently gained by making the surface smaller is lost on account of the greater pressure between each point, and the total friction remains the same.

146. We learn from this that (so far as friction is concerned) there is no advantage in narrow runners over broad ones for a sledge or a skate; or in broad rims for the driving-wheel of a locomotive engine, where the object is to have as much friction on the rail as possible. A box requires as much force to drag

it along a floor, whether it is lying flat or resting on one corner only.

Coefficient of Friction.

147. From the experiments made to illustrate Law IV., it will be seen that the force required to overcome the friction between two surfaces is always *the same fraction* of the pressure existing between the surfaces, whatever that pressure is. Thus, if a wooden box weighs 10 lbs., and if 3 lbs. are required to keep it moving over a wooden floor, then we may state the friction as being $\frac{3}{10}$ of the pressure. If the box weighs 20 lbs., a force of 6 lbs. will be required to keep it moving; but 6 lbs. is $\frac{6}{20}$ or $\frac{3}{10}$ of the pressure—that is, the same fraction as in the former case. Hence we can conveniently and accurately express the amount of friction between two surfaces by stating once for all what fraction of the whole pressure between the surfaces is required to overcome it. This fraction is called the 'Coefficient of Friction,' and its approximate value for different substances is given in the table below.

Table of Coefficients of Friction.

[The figure means the fraction of the total pressure between the surfaces which is required to overcome the friction when they are moving over one another.]

Iron and Sandstone..........$\frac{5}{10}$	Metal and Metal..........$\frac{2}{10}$
Wood and Metal..........$\frac{4}{10}$	Grease and Grease (less than).$\frac{1}{10}$
Wood and Wood..........$\frac{3}{10}$	

Methods of lessening Friction.

148. For many purposes we want to get rid of friction as much as possible, since force has to be spent in overcoming it, and various means may be employed for this object.

(1) The surfaces should be made of those materials between which the least friction is found to exist.

(2) They should be made as smooth as possible. Thus, highly polished surfaces of steel working on bearings of brass or bronze are employed in machinery. In watches the delicate steel pivots work in polished holes cut in rubies or sapphires, or similar extremely hard 'jewels.'

(3) They should be covered with oil or grease. Then, whatever

the material below may be, the friction is between surfaces of oil only, and this (as the above table shows) is very small. This is one of the most general and effective methods of preventing friction, and is employed in addition to the other means above mentioned. The bearings of machinery usually have oil-cups fitted to them, from which the lubricating substance is constantly supplied to the moving parts. More than a gallon of oil is thus consumed in every locomotive engine in running 200 miles, while no less than 100 gallons of lubricants are required *per diem* in the powerful machinery of the large steamers which cross the Atlantic.*

(4) The surfaces may be made to roll over one another instead of sliding. Thus, in moving large blocks of stone along the floor of a quarry, a couple of rollers are put under the stone, as shown in fig. 19, and the heavy mass is then easily pushed forwards. As one of the rollers comes out behind in the course of the movement, another is put in front; and thus immense blocks can be transferred from place to place by the use of a very small force. In fact, friction (strictly so called) may by this expedient be abolished altogether.

Fig. 19.

149. The employment of wheels for carriages depends upon the same principle, the force required to draw a carriage being far less than that which would be wanted for a sledge of the same weight. Thus the coefficient of friction (as it may still be called, for convenience) for a carriage on a well-made level road is $\frac{1}{30}$; while on a railway, or a good tramway, it is only $\frac{1}{280}$ for moderate speeds. For example, a carriage weighing 1 ton requires, to drag it at a moderate speed along a good road, $\frac{1}{30}$ of a ton, or 74 lbs.; to drag it along a railway only $\frac{1}{280}$ of a ton, or 8 lbs. are required.†

* These figures are given on excellent authority, and show what is required even with rigid economy. The expense of merely lessening friction by lubrication in a passenger engine amounts to nearly £20 a year.

† At high speeds the resistance of the air becomes a serious obstacle, so that the coefficient is $\frac{1}{70}$ or more (about 30 lbs. per ton) for a train running 60 miles an hour.

150. The reasons why, after inertia has been overcome, force has to be continually supplied in order to keep up the motion of a wheel carriage, are mainly the following:

(1) *Adhesion or cohesion between the edge of the wheel and the road.* This has to be overcome when each point of the wheel or roller is lifted up from the road as it moves on.

(2) *Imperfect hardness of the road or wheel, or both.*—The effect of this is that the surface gives way more or less under the pressure, so that the wheel is always in a hollow, and therefore as it moves on it has continually to push down the higher part in front of it; and force must, of course, be spent in doing this. It is easy to observe how much even a massive steel rail yields under the pressure of a passing train; and the ruts in a road are a permanent record of the expenditure of force in the above way.

(3) *Sliding friction at the axle of the wheel.*—The whole weight of the carriage acts between the axle and its bearing, and between the edge of the wheel and the road. As the carriage moves on, each point in the edge of the wheel is held by the friction on the road, so that the whole wheel moves round and the bearing slides upon the axle. The friction between these latter surfaces is the full amount due to the weight of the carriage, but the force which overcomes it is applied at the edge of the wheel—that is, at the end of the long arm of a lever formed by each radius or spoke of the wheel; and so this force acts with greater advantage (as will be more fully explained under the head of LEVERS) than if it was applied at the point where the bearing and the axle are in contact. Thus, the effect of the sliding friction at the axle in resisting the motion of the carriage, is much less than it would be if the axle rested on the road; and it is less in proportion as the arm of the lever—that is, the length of the radius or spoke of the wheel—is longer. Hence we see why carriages with large wheels are easier to draw than those with smaller ones.

151. It is possible to lessen materially, and almost abolish, sliding friction at the axle in the following ways:

(1) Two wheels are placed close to each other in a frame, as shown in fig. 20, with their edges overlapping. The axle rests on their edges, and turns them round as it moves, rolling

instead of sliding on their surfaces. Thus the sliding friction is only that of the supporting wheels on their axles; and this is comparatively small, as above explained. The figure shows how this principle is applied in supporting the pulley of an apparatus called Attwood's machine, used in experiments on the Laws of Motion; and large grindstones are often mounted in a similar way. Such pairs of wheels are called 'friction wheels.'

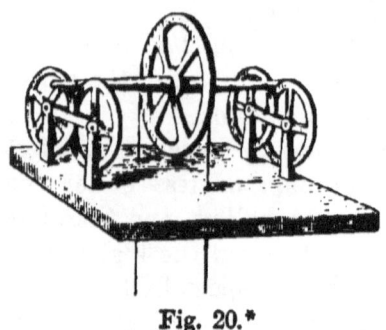

Fig. 20.*

(2) A number of accurately-made hard steel balls are placed in a circular recess surrounding the axle, which rests on their surfaces, and rolls them round in the box as it rotates. Such arrangements are called 'ball-bearings,' and are extensively used in bicycles.

152. Before passing on, we may consider for a moment the advantages and disadvantages of friction. It is a phenomenon which meets us everywhere. Whenever we try to make a body move, not only has its inertia to be overcome, but some force has always and continuously to be expended in overcoming friction; so that we can never, however perfect a machine may be, get the full theoretical effect of a force in useful work. Every movement of our bodies implies friction at each joint, although nature has supplied a wonderfully efficient lubricating apparatus and material wherever it is needed.† In rowing, we find friction at the rowlock, and a considerable amount of it at the sliding-seat.

153. Not only is force thus wasted, but the surfaces in contact soon wear away, particles being constantly torn off owing to the friction. Hence, bearings of machinery soon work loose and have to be renewed; boots and clothes wear out; and a little dust becomes an interesting study under the microscope, from the variety of materials which friction has contributed to it.

---

* From Prof. Balfour Stewart's *Elementary Physics*.

† Any injury to these 'synovial membranes,' as they are called, results in a permanent stiffness of the joint.

154. Yet we must not think that friction is universally harmful, or even useless. We could not, in the most literal sense of the words, 'get on' without it. The friction between our feet and the ground enables us to walk or run onward, as any one will soon find out if he tries to walk or run on ice with skates on. Window-blinds are raised and lowered by the friction of the cord upon the pulley at the end of the blind-roller; and machinery in a mill is often worked by leather straps passing with great friction over pulleys on a shaft turned by the engine. A railway train is moved on by the friction between the driving-wheels of the engine and the rails; it is stopped by the friction between the brake and the wheels. If the rails are from any cause greasy, the driver soon finds that the engine is powerless to draw the train owing to the wheels slipping; sand is then scattered on the rails, which increases the friction until the driving-wheels again 'bite' on the rail.

155. Friction, again, contributes immensely to the stability of things. Without it, furniture, books, &c. would be continually slipping about, like dead leaves before a breath of wind. India-rubber is chosen for the soles of racquet- and fives- shoes because of the high coefficient of friction between it and stone. It is owing to friction that nails and screws stick so firmly in wood, and that secure knots can be tied in string or rope. Even the wear and tear produced by it are made to serve a useful purpose. Most cleaning and polishing operations depend on friction; knives, &c. are sharpened on a grindstone; corn is ground to flour in a mill.

Section 4.—The Second Law of Motion.

The momentum produced by a force is exactly proportional to the magnitude of the force; and when several forces act on a body, each produces motion in its own direction, just as if it was the only force acting.

156. We have in this law two distinct statements as to the action of forces, which must be considered separately.

A. Momentum varies exactly with the force which produces it.

Thus, if a cricket-ball weighing $\frac{1}{4}$ lb. is thrown with a force which gives it a velocity of 12 feet per second, its momentum will, of course, be ($\frac{1}{3} \times 12 =$) 4; now, if we find that the ball has twice this momentum, we know that exactly twice as much force must have been exerted in throwing it; similarly, three times the force will give it three times the momentum, and so on.

157. This fact is of great use in the exact comparison and measurement of forces; for if we want to find out how much one force is greater than another, we have only to make each of them act for the same time upon the same body, and observe how much momentum each produces. If one force gives ten times as much momentum as the other, then although we cannot catch a glimpse of the forces themselves, we are sure (from the above law) that the former force must be of ten times the magnitude.

158. In expressing the magnitude of forces we must begin by choosing some particular amount of force, to be taken as the 'unit' or standard; just as a gramme or a pound is fixed upon as a unit of weight, and a metre or a foot as the unit of length. Then we can always give an exact idea of the magnitude of any given force by saying that it is so many units. The unit of force adopted in England is called a '**poundal**,' and is

That amount of force which, acting for 1 second on a mass of 1 pound, gives it a velocity of 1 foot per second.

159. It is easily seen from the above definition that a poundal of force, when applied to a body for 1 second of time, gives it a momentum of 1 in terms of lbs. ft. sec.; so that, by finding the momentum of a body in terms of these units, we at once learn what impulse in poundals has been applied to it. Suppose, for instance, that a football weighing $\frac{1}{2}$ lb. is moving, directly after being kicked, with a speed of 20 feet per second. Then its momentum is, of course ($\frac{1}{2} \times 20 =$) 10, and hence the amount of impulse given it by the kick was equivalent to 10 poundals of force. Again, if we allow a stone which has a mass of 1 lb. to fall freely for exactly 1 second, we find that at the end of the second it has acquired a velocity of 32 feet per second (nearly). Hence its momentum is ($1 \times 32 =$) 32; and therefore the magnitude of gravitation-force in England is 32

poundals. Similarly, supposing that an eight-oar racing-boat weighs with the crew on board 1800 lbs., and that 1 second after starting it is found to be moving at the rate of 8 feet per second. Then its momentum is (8 × 1800 =) 14,400; and the crew must have exerted 14,400 poundals of force in the first second after the start.

B. Every force acts independently of others.

160. A force is, as it were, an absolutely selfish but conscientious individual, which doggedly does its own proper share of work, and neither more nor less, totally regardless of the interruptions or solicitations of other forces. For instance, the earth and all things upon it are (as already mentioned, p. 38) in rapid motion, and yet we find that we can move about and move other things about just as well as if the earth was not moving at all; in fact, the forces which we apply act quite independently of the earth's motions.

161. If a ball is let fall from the top of the mast of a ship, it will strike the deck at the bottom of the mast in just the same place whether the ship is motionless at anchor, or is in swift but steady motion. In the latter case there are, at the moment when it is let fall, two forces acting upon the ball: (1) gravitation pulling it downwards; (2) the force of the wind or the steam, which is moving it, and everything else connected with the ship, onwards. After it has begun to fall, the latter force ceases to act, but the onward motion which it has communicated to the ball continues (according to Law I.); so that by the time the ball reaches the deck it has gone as far forward as the deck itself has. So, again, a juggler finds that in tossing up balls and catching them again, he has to move his hands in precisely the same direction whether he is standing still or is on the back of a galloping horse; for in the latter case the necessary onward motion of the balls is supplied without any effort on his part, so that they keep up with him and fall into his hands again just as if he was standing still. When a bar is held in his way above the horse, he does not require to leap forward in surmounting it; he springs directly upwards, and this upward motion, combined with the forward motion he has in common with the horse, results in carrying him in a curve over the

obstacle, and planting him on the very spot of the horse's back he sprang from.

162. The above principle is of extreme importance in enabling us to find the exact direction in which a body will move when (not one, but) *several* forces act on it. This would be a most complicated problem if we had to allow in every case for the influence of one force upon another in modifying its effect; but as it is, we can consider the velocity and direction imparted by each force quite irrespective of the others, with perfect certainty that this velocity and direction will appear unaltered in the final result.

Section 5.—Composition of Forces.

163. This means the examination of the combined effect of several forces which act on a point in the same body, in order to find a single force which will produce the same effect as all of them. **Resultant** is the term applied to such a single force which is equivalent to several others; and the separate forces to which it is equivalent are called its **components**. We shall consider three separate cases of the composition of forces, and show how the principle of Law II. is applied in each of them.

164. It may be noted here that, since the forces are considered in their action on the *same* body, the mass of which is unaltered during their action, their relative magnitudes may be quite correctly expressed by simply stating the velocity (and not the momentum) which each would produce in the body. Thus, if a cricket-ball is hit by one player with a force which makes it move 10 feet per second, and the same ball is hit by another player with a force which makes it move 30 feet per second, we know that the latter force must be three times as great as the former, without regarding the weight of the ball. So in many subsequent examples the forces will be expressed by stating the velocity they produce in the body on which they act.

A. When the forces act in the same direction on a point in a body.

165. Here, since each force produces its own proper effect, and neither more nor less, we have only to add the magnitudes

of the forces together. The sum of these magnitudes is the required resultant, and it acts, of course, in the same direction as each and all of its components.

166. For example, when a team of horses is drawing a waggon, the resultant force applied to the waggon is the sum of the separate efforts of each horse. When a barge is towed by a steam-tug along a river *with* the stream, the resultant speed of the barge is that which would be communicated to it by the stream alone added to that which the steamer itself imparts.

B. When two forces act in opposite directions on a point in a body.

167. In this case we must subtract the magnitude of the smaller force from that of the greater; the remainder will be the magnitude of the resultant, and it will act in the direction of the greater force.

168. Suppose, for instance, that a steam-tug is towing a barge *against* the stream of a river. Then the resultant force on the barge, as shown by the speed it goes, will be the difference between the force of the stream and the force of the tug. If the stream alone would carry on the barge at the rate of 2 miles per hour, while the steamer alone would drag it along at the rate of 7 miles per hour on a canal or lake, the actual resultant speed of the barge will be (7 − 2 =) 5 miles per hour up the river.

169. The same applies, of course, to rowing on a river: the rate of progress of a boat up-stream is the difference between the speed due to the current and that due to the force applied by the rowers.* Again, in football, if two players urge the ball in opposite directions, the actual effect on the ball is the difference between the forces they apply respectively.

170. A good example of both the above cases of the composition of forces is afforded by the game called the 'tug of war,' or 'French and English.' In it two sets of players endeavour to drag a rope in opposite directions; and the resultant force with which the rope moves is found by (1) adding together the forces

---

* It is said to be harder to row against the stream, not necessarily because more labour is expended by the rowers in each stroke, but because more strokes are needed to carry the boat through a given distance.

of the separate players on each side, (2) subtracting the smaller sum from the greater; the remainder expresses the resultant force with which the rope and the weaker set of players clinging to it will be dragged over the 'scratch' line.

C. When two forces act in directions which make an angle (other than 180°) with each other.

171. This is a rather more difficult case. Suppose a ball is rolling along a table or a cricket-field, and it is hit sideways, in what direction will it thenceforwards move?

172. It is necessary in the first place to attend to the distinction between motion *in the same direction* and motion *in the same straight line*. In a regiment of soldiers on the march, each man is moving in the same direction, northwards for instance, though he is not moving in the same straight line as those on his right and left. Now, when a force has produced motion in its own direction, it has done its proper work, whether the movement be in the same straight line or not. In fig. 21 the ball B is moving in the same direction, whether it move in the line AC or in any line parallel to AC, as *gf* or ED; in any of these cases it is equally approaching the line CD. In the same way a motion from B towards E, or from *h* towards *i*, or from C towards D, is still in the same direction, because these lines are parallel.

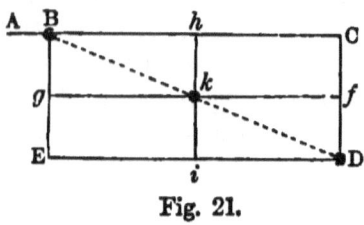

Fig. 21.

173. Now, let the ball be moving along the line AC with a velocity that would carry it from B to C in two seconds, and when at B let it receive a blow that would carry it from B to E in the same time; the question is, How will the ball now move? This is best understood by supposing it placed, not on a plane surface, but in a groove in the upper side of a movable bar lying on a table. The ball being now set rolling at the same rate as before along a groove in the bar AC, let the bar be made at the same time to slide across the table, keeping parallel to itself, and carrying the ball along with it, so as to arrive at the position ED in two seconds. The common motion of the bar and the ball will not in any way interfere with the motion of

the ball in the groove, any more than the common motion of a ship and a man on board of it interferes with the man in walking across the deck. The ball will be at the end of the groove at the end of the two seconds, just as if the bar had been at rest; it will therefore, as a result of the two movements, be found at the point D.

174. If the position of the ball on the table is observed at the intermediate points, it will be found to describe a straight line from B to D; for since we have supposed both motions uniform, the bar will, at the end of the first second, be in the position gf, midway between BC and ED, and the ball will at the same instant be half-way from g to f, at k; and it can be proved (Euclid, VI. 26) that k is in a straight line between B and D. The same could be shown as to any intermediate stage.—When both motions are not uniform, the body moves in a curve, as is the case with projectiles.

175. The movable groove is introduced to make the effect of two movements conjoined more readily conceived; to show palpably, as it were, that a body may be moving in two directions at one and the same time. But if it receive the second impulse by a blow while rolling freely on the table, it will still arrive at D by the same path.

176. Now, since ED is parallel to BC, and CD is parallel to BE, the figure BCDE is a parallelogram (Euclid, I. Definitions), two adjacent sides of which, such as BE and BC, represent respectively the two forces which act on the body A. Further, a line drawn from B to D is called a 'diagonal' of the parallelogram; and it has been shown to represent accurately, both in magnitude and direction, the resultant of the two forces BC and BE. Such a figure is called a **parallelogram of forces**.

177. It will now be seen how easily we can, by drawing such a figure correctly to scale, find out quite accurately the magnitude and direction of any two forces which act at any angle upon a point in a body. We must do as follows:

Through the point at which the forces act draw lines, AB, AC, fig. 22 (next page), to represent each force in direction and magnitude; taking the lengths on any convenient scale of equal parts, such as centimetres or inches.

Through the outer ends of each, B and C, draw a line parallel to the other force, namely, BD and CD, so as to make a parallelogram.

Through the point at which the forces act draw a diagonal, AD, of the parallelogram.

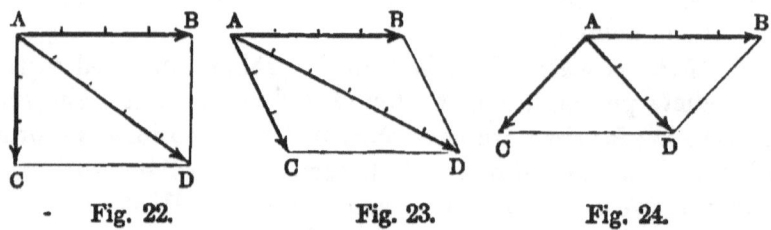

Fig. 22.   Fig. 23.   Fig. 24.

Then this diagonal will represent the resultant of the two forces, both in direction and magnitude.

[The student should notice how the value of the resultant changes with the angle between the component forces. In the above figures the components have the same value—namely, AB = 4 units, AC = 3 units, but the magnitude and direction of the resultant is very different. In fig. 23, for instance, it is 6 units, while in fig. 24 it is only 3 units, owing to the wide angle between the directions of the components. The wider this angle, the more nearly the forces act against one another, and when it is 180° the resultant is only equal to the difference between the forces, as already stated.]

178. We may next take some practical examples of the composition of forces; and for simplicity we shall consider only cases where there are two forces acting at right angles,* and we shall take the velocity produced by the forces to express their respective magnitudes, as explained in par. 164.

179. Suppose that a ferry-boat is being rowed across a river with a force which gives it a speed of 4 miles an hour; and meanwhile the current is carrying it down the river at the rate of 3 miles an hour. It is plain that the boat will not go straight across the river, but in a slanting direction, so as to reach the opposite side at a place farther down the river than the point directly opposite its starting-place. The exact direction and

---

* If there are more than two forces concerned, first the resultant of any two of them is found as above, and then this resultant is combined with another of the forces, and the resultant of this pair is found, and so on.

speed of the boat may be found by the 'parallelogram of forces,' thus: Draw (as in fig. 25) a line, AB, 4 units long (on any scale, such as one of centimetres or inches) to represent the force of the rowers. Through A draw a line AC, 3 units long (on the same scale) to represent the force of the current. Complete the parallelogram ACDB, and through A draw a diagonal AD. Then this diagonal will represent the direction in which the boat will actually move; and it will be found to be just 5 units long.

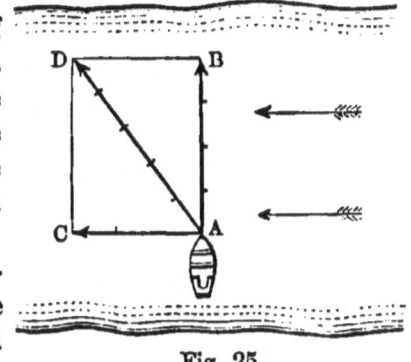

Fig. 25.

Therefore the boat will move in the direction A to D with a force which gives it a speed of 5 miles an hour.

180. Again, suppose that a cricket-ball, bowled with a force of 50 poundals, is hit in the direction of square-leg with a force of 120 poundals. Then, drawing a parallelogram as above described, with sides of 50 and 120 units (a millimetre scale may be used), we shall find that the diagonal is 130 units long. Thus the ball will travel more nearly in the direction of long-leg, and with a force of 130 poundals.

181. Many other examples of the composition of forces will suggest themselves; such as, a ball thrown at the wicket by a player while running, a shot fired from a moving ship at a battery on shore, a boat towed along a river by two men, one on each bank.

Section 6.—Resolution of Forces.

182. This is the exact converse of the composition of forces, and means the division of one force into several others, called its 'components,' which, taken together, are equivalent to it.

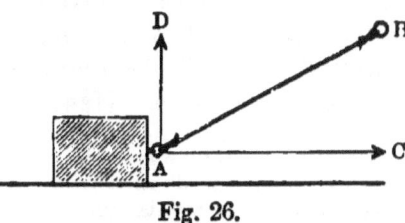

Fig. 26.

183. For instance, if a man is dragging a block of stone along the ground by a rope slanting

upwards from it to his hand, as shown in fig. 26, the single force, AB, which he applies along the rope and in its direction, is really equivalent to, and might be replaced by, two forces, AC and AD, one of which tends to raise the block of stone directly from the ground, while the other alone is effective in dragging it along the ground.

184. The magnitude of these two components can easily be found by constructing a parallelogram of forces. To do this, we must consider the single original force as a diagonal, round which we have, as it were, to fit a parallelogram; and the adjacent sides of this will represent the component forces required.

185. It is evident that we must know the directions which the two components are to have.* Suppose that the total force applied to the rope is 8 poundals, and that we want to find how much of it is spent in dragging the stone along, and how much is spent in merely raising it from the ground. The directions of the components will then be at right angles to each other, as in the figure.

186. Make the line AB, fig. 27, 8 units long, and through A draw two lines of any length, AX horizontal, and AY vertical; these lines will then represent the *directions* of the required components, and we have to find what lengths must be cut off from them to represent correctly the magnitudes.

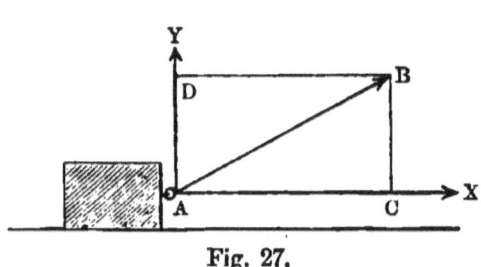

Fig. 27.

Through B draw BC parallel to AD, and also BD parallel to AC. Then ACBD is a parallelogram, for its opposite sides are parallel; and two of its adjacent sides, AC and AD, represent correctly two forces, which are together equivalent to the single force AB. If these two sides are measured, AC will be found almost exactly 7 units, and AD 4 units of the scale. Hence we learn that 7 poundals of force

---

* Or, of course, their magnitudes, in which case their directions may be found; or the magnitude and direction of one of them, in which case the magnitude and direction of the other may be found.

are being spent in moving the stone onward, and 4 poundals in raising it upward, or at any rate lessening the pressure between it and the ground.

[Several similar figures should be drawn, with the direction of the rope—that is, the diagonal of the parallelogram—more or less inclined to the horizontal line of the ground; and the effect on the relative magnitudes of the components should be noted.]

187. When a barge is being towed along a river or canal by a horse on the bank, the force exerted through the tow-rope is not all effective in moving the barge onwards. It may, in fact, as shown in fig. 28, be resolved into two components, AC and AD, at right angles to one another; one of which, AC, moves the boat straight along the river, while the other, AD, only tends to pull it towards the bank. Suppose, for instance, that the horse is pulling with a force of 85 poundals in the direction AB. Make AB 85 units long; then, on constructing the parallelogram, it will be found that AC represents a force of 84 poundals, and AD one of 13 poundals. In order to counteract this latter component, and prevent the boat being dragged into the bank, the rudder must be used; and its action supplies another rather more complicated example of the resolution of forces, which will be further explained in the appendix to this chapter.

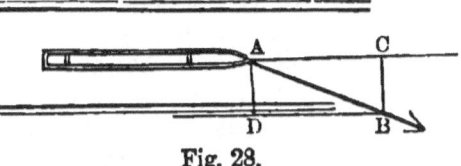

Fig. 28.

188. Other good examples of the resolution of a force in such a way that it seems to act in a direction other than its own, are afforded by the action of a horizontally-blowing wind on a kite so as to cause it to rise vertically in the air; the action of a wind blowing across the course of a ship on sails set obliquely to the keel (a north wind, for instance, impelling the ship along a westerly or even north-westerly course); the effect of a wind on the sails of a windmill. In all these cases two distinct processes of resolution have to be performed; the final result being, that a certain amount of the force appears as a component which acts in a direction making a right angle, or even a greater angle, with that of the original force.

APPENDIX.

Action of the rudder in altering the course of a ship.

189. The rudder is a flat plate, hinged vertically to the stern of the ship, so that it can swing from side to side like a door. When its surface, or 'plane,' is in the same line as the keel, it merely acts as a portion of the keel, and steadies the ship in the course in which she is going. But when it is turned at all obliquely to the right or left of the line of the keel, it and the sternpost to which it is hinged undergo a pressure in the opposite direction. Thus in fig. 28, the rudder has been moved to the *left* of the line of the keel; hence the stern of the ship is pushed to the *right* hand, and therefore the bow points to the left of its former course, and so the whole vessel proceeds in that direction. The question is, how does the rudder get this pressure sideways?

As the ship moves on, the inertia of the water-particles which the rudder meets causes them to press against its surface in the direction AB, fig. 29. Now, AB may be resolved into two

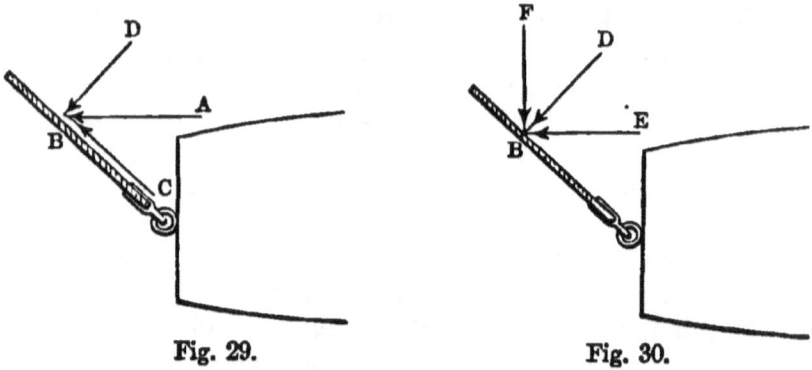

Fig. 29.   Fig. 30.

components at right angles to each other—namely, CB, which is parallel to the surface of the rudder, and therefore has no effect on it at all, and DB, which presses at right angles to the surface.

190. Let us next take this latter component DB as a distinct force (see fig. 30). It may be resolved into two components at right angles to each other—namely, EB, which simply presses the rudder in the contrary direction to that in which the ship is going, and thus retards the whole ship; and FB, which pushes the rudder sideways, and therefore the stern of the ship also. It is this latter

component alone which is effective in changing the course of the ship, which it does in the manner above explained.

191. The calculation of the action of the wind on sails of a ship, or on a kite, referred to in par. 188, p. 75, is made on exactly the same principle as above described—namely, to resolve the force of the wind into two components, one of which is at right angles to the sail or kite, and then to resolve this latter force into two others, one of which urges the ship on, or raises the kite upwards. It will be a useful exercise to work out these problems more fully from the hints just given.

Section 7.—The Third Law of Motion.

The action of a force is always accompanied by a reaction in the body to which it is applied. This reaction is equal to the force in magnitude, and is in the opposite direction.

192. When a football is kicked, it presses against the foot with just as much force as the foot presses against it. When one stone is dashed against another stone at rest, the moving stone is hit as hard, and is as likely to break, as the one at rest; and when one person knocks his head against his neighbour's, it is difficult to say which is most hurt. The hand pressed against a fixed body is equally pressed in its turn. If a man standing in a boat attempts to push off another boat of the same weight that is alongside, both boats will recede equally from each other; if he pulls the other boat towards him, his own boat advances half-way to meet it. A magnet draws a piece of iron towards it; but the magnet is also drawn towards the iron, as is seen when they are both suspended so as to move freely. In all these cases we see that the body which we consider as acting upon the other, is itself acted upon in turn, and in the opposite direction: this is what is meant by *reaction*. But to determine more exactly the equality of the action and reaction in all cases, it is necessary to advert to the way in which action is measured.

193. In all cases of the action of a force there are two portions of matter concerned—(A) the one in which the force is considered to reside; (B) the one on which it is considered to act. Thus, in the action between a magnet and a piece of iron, the force of attraction is considered to reside in the magnet, and the

piece of iron is usually only considered as being attracted. Hitherto we have hardly considered A except as the vehicle, as it were, of the force; but in point of fact, as the above examples show, just as much effect is produced on it during the action of the force, as on B. Now, as we have seen already, p. 41, the effect of a force is estimated, not alone by the *velocity* it produces, but by taking into consideration also the *mass* on which it acts. Mass multiplied by velocity—that is, the **momentum produced**—is the true measure of the force which has acted on a body; and what the third law of motion asserts is this: That in any case of the action of a force, just as much momentum is produced in the body in which it is considered to reside, as in the body on which it acts; but this momentum is in the opposite direction.

194. To recur to the examples of reaction formerly cited. If the magnet and the piece of iron are of the same weight, they move to meet each other with equal velocities, for thus only can the momentum be the same in both cases. If the magnet is three times the weight of the piece of iron, the iron must move with three times the velocity of the magnet to make the momentum the same; and so it is found to do. In the case of the boats, suppose the one in which the man is seated to be ten times the weight of the other, then for every ten feet that the light one moves off, the heavy one will recede one foot; so that the two will have the same momentum.

195. In the last case, both motions would still be visible. But let a boat of a ton weight be pushed away from the side of a ship of one thousand tons weight, and then only one seems to move; for while the boat moves off a yard, the ship recedes only the thousandth part of a yard, which it would require minute observation and measurement to render apparent. From this we can pass to the extreme case of a boat pushed off from shore. Where is the evidence of reaction here? We see none, it is true; still, the consideration of the cases already adduced, and of a thousand similar, lead us irresistibly to believe that the shore, if it is free to move, must recede from the boat. But the shore can move only by carrying the earth with it; and considering the vast mass of the earth compared with that of the boat, the space moved over would defy measurement, even if

we had any fixed mark to count from. We cannot help believing, then, that when a stone falls—in other words, when the earth draws a stone towards it—the earth is itself drawn, or falls, towards the stone.

196. Other examples of the equality of action and reaction are the following: When a spring is compressed, although the compressing force is only applied at one end, yet there is produced in every part of the spring a strain which shows itself as a force acting in two opposite directions; so that the spring may be used to propel a bullet either in the direction of the compressing force, or in the opposite direction.

197. Similarly, when a gun is fired, the gases suddenly produced in the breech act like a strongly compressed spring, and exercise pressure, not only against the bullet, but also against the closed end of the gun. The result is not only that the bullet is driven out with great velocity, but also that the whole mass of the gun is driven in the opposite direction with an exactly equal momentum. This explains the recoil or 'kick' of the gun against the shoulder. For instance, the weight of an army rifle is 10 lbs., and the bullet weighs about $1\frac{1}{3}$ oz. ($\frac{1}{12}$ lb.); that is, the gun is 120 times as heavy as the bullet. Now, suppose that the bullet is driven out with a velocity of 1200 feet per second; then its momentum is ($1200 \times \frac{1}{12}$ lbs. $=$) 100. And the gun will recoil with a momentum equal to this; but since its weight is 120 times that of the bullet, its velocity will be 120 times less; that is ($\frac{1}{120}$ of $1200 =$) 10 feet per second. In order to avoid the consequences of this recoil, the carriages of large guns are made very massive, and are allowed to run back up an incline and checked by ropes or hydraulic buffers. Still, cases have been known of a gun being fairly shot away from its carriage, and doing much damage in its backward course.

To illustrate roughly some of the facts of action and reaction, an apparatus made on the principle of a common toy spring-gun (or one of the actual toys slightly altered) is convenient. The spring, when compressed, should be held by a loop of thread hung over a hook attached to the gun; a pencil or a bit of iron rod being put into the barrel as a projectile. The gun is then laid on a smooth table, and the spring released by burning the thread with a lighted match. As an extreme case, the projectile may be made of the same weight as the gun, and the distance travelled by each from the starting-point (that is, the point where the projectile is in contact with the spring within the barrel) may be measured.*

198. Another interesting example of reaction is a rocket. Here the gun is actually used as the projectile; a constant stream of particles of gas is rushing with immense velocity from the mouth of the rocket, and the latter recoils with an equal momentum.

199. In rowing, the feet always rest against a cross-piece or 'stretcher,' firmly attached to the boat. But they do not merely rest against it; they press against it with the same force as that which is applied to the oar; and for the following reason : When the oar is pulled by the hands, it pulls (owing to reaction) against the hands with an equal force; and the body would be pulled up to the oar, if it were not that the feet, set rigidly against the stretcher, prevent this movement, so that the force of the muscles is only operative in pulling the oar up to the body. It is well known in rowing that, unless a rower is 'feeling his stretcher'—that is, is exerting consciously a pressure against it—he cannot be doing any useful work.

200. In the case of a carriage being run away with, persons riding in it have been known to lay hold of the sides to hold it back: they forget that, while pulling back with their hands, they are pushing forwards with their feet, and that the action and reaction, being equal and contrary, destroy each other's effects.

Section 8.—Collision of Bodies.

201. When one moving body strikes against another body, which either is at rest, or is moving in a different direction, or is moving in the same direction but with a different velocity, the two are said to 'come into collision.' Such common examples will suggest themselves as collisions between two trains or ships; the striking of a cricket-ball against a bat, of a fives-ball against the walls or floor of the court, of a billiard-ball against another ball, or against the cushion of the table. In all such cases there

---

* It should, of course, be observed that these distances express energy, and not merely momentum, as will be more fully explained in a later chapter.

is invariably some change in the motion of the bodies; and the nature of the change will be easily understood if we bear in mind the principle (to be more fully explained in the chapter on Energy and Work), that *no force whatever is under any circumstances actually created or destroyed in the universe, so far as we know it;* so that, when momentum is communicated from one body to another, the original amount of momentum, and neither more nor less, remains in the whole mass affected, though its distribution may be different. This is the general law, but the results actually observable are dependent on the amount of elasticity of the substances concerned—that is, upon the extent to which their molecules endeavour to recover their original positions when a pressure or strain has been put upon them.

(A) **Collision of non-elastic bodies.**

202. Suppose that a piece of soft moist clay or of lead (bodies of which the elasticity is very slight) weighing 12 lbs., is driven, with a velocity of 10 feet per sec., against a similar piece weighing 4 lbs., which is at rest. The momentum of the first mass is obviously ($12 \times 10 =$) **120**. Now, the first effect of the action and reaction is to compress the molecules of both pieces until their cohesion balances the force, and in this way some of the force associated with the moving body is spent, which we may express by a loss of momentum of, say, 20. The next effect is, that the masses move on in contact with a momentum which is equal to all that remains of the original momentum of the striking body, that is, ($120 - 20 =$) **100**. But the velocity of the united mass must clearly be less than 10 feet per sec., since the mass in motion is now ($12 + 4 =$) 16 lbs., instead of only 12 lbs. The velocity in feet per sec. will, in fact, be represented by such a number as will, when multiplied by 16, give a product of 100; and this is, of course, the quotient of 100 divided by 16—namely, $6\frac{1}{4}$. So that the observed effect will be, that the two masses will move on together with a velocity of $6\frac{1}{4}$ feet per sec. in the same direction as the heavier body was originally moving.

203. If the bodies which come into collision are both in motion but in opposite directions—for instance, two football

players charging each other—the result will depend upon their relative momenta. If their momenta are equal, the reaction of each destroys the motion of the other, and they are both brought to rest. If their momenta are different, then they move on in contact after the collision, in the direction in which that body was moving which had the greater momentum.

204. Suppose, for example, that a player weighing 140 lbs., and moving 10 feet per sec., charges another weighing 100 lbs., and moving 9 ft. per sec. Then the momentum of the first is $(140 \times 10 =)$ **1400**; and that of the second is $(100 \times 9 =)$ **900**. When they come in contact, the momentum of the lighter player, namely, 900, counteracts an equivalent amount of the momentum of the heavier one; so that the remaining momentum is $(1400 - 900 =)$ **500**. Of this we may suppose 20 lost in compression of the molecules, &c., leaving 480 remaining. This 480 is the momentum of the whole mass of $(140 + 100 =)$ 240 lbs. So the velocity will be only $(\frac{480}{240} =)$ 2 feet per sec., and the motion will be in the direction in which the first player was running; in fact he will overpower the other and press him back.

(B) **Collision of elastic bodies.**

205. This is by far the most usual case; few, if any, substances being quite destitute of elasticity. Suppose, for instance, that an ivory ball strikes another similar ball of the same weight. The first effect of the collision is, as already stated, to compress the molecules of both balls, and alter their position against the force of their cohesion. In this, no force is lost as mechanical force (as with non-elastic bodies, in which the cohesion has no power to bring back the molecules to their places), but is stored up as in a compressed spring. In the next place, this force of cohesion exerts itself, and the balls are pushed apart with equal momenta in opposite directions. The result is, (1) that the ball which was originally moving, being met by an equal and opposite force, has its motion stopped entirely; (2) that the other ball is set in motion with the same velocity (since it is of equal weight) as that of the ball which struck it.

[To show this, two ivory billiard-balls (stone balls will answer, but not so well) may be hung by strings from a frame, fig. 31, so as to be just in contact. One of them is then drawn aside, and allowed to swing against the other, which immediately moves onward (the first ball remaining stationary), and may be caught before it swings back.]

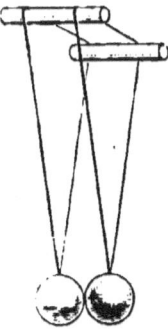

Fig. 31.

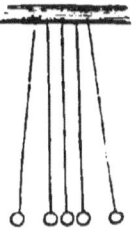

Fig. 32.

206. This peculiar action of elastic bodies appears when a number of ivory balls are placed close in a row, and the outermost at one end is smartly struck against the next; none of them move sensibly from their places, except the outermost at the other end of the row. Each ball in turn receives the whole motion from the one that precedes it, and gives it away entire to the next. The last becomes thus the vehicle of the whole motion. Instead of placing the balls on a table, they may be suspended as in fig. 32.

207. If the striking ball is heavier than the other, the momentum generated during the spring-action above explained is not sufficient to stop its onward motion, but only to lessen it. This is what usually occurs when a cricket-bat or a golf-club hits the ball. The bat or club still moves onward after the ball is hit,* but a comparatively small effort on the part of the striker is sufficient to stop it. If the ball is missed, the consequences are unpleasantly felt: the bat moves on with undiminished momentum, and may be flung, as it were, out of the player's hand.

SECTION 9.—LAWS OF REFLEXION.

208. When a body strikes a fixed surface, if both are completely inelastic, its motion is destroyed and it remains on the surface. But this is true only of soft masses; all hard solids have more or less elasticity, and rebound or are *reflected* from the surface, and this reflexion follows a regular law of direction. If an ivory ball, for instance, be dropped, as from L, fig. 33, on a level marble slab at K, it will rebound in the same perpendicular

---

* Unless, of course, the ball itself is bowled so swiftly against the bat as to supply a sufficient momentum on its own account.

line, and, being almost perfectly elastic, will rise again nearly to L. But if the ball is thrown obliquely in the direction H to K, the action and reaction drive it back in a direction KI, which makes the same angle with the perpendicular KL, drawn to the surface where the ball hits it, as the original direction of the ball made with this perpendicular. In fact, the angle HKL, which is called the 'angle of incidence,' is always found to be equal to the angle LKI, which is called the 'angle of reflexion.' Moreover, the direction of incidence, HK; the direction of reflexion, KI; and the perpendicular, KL, always lie in the same plane.

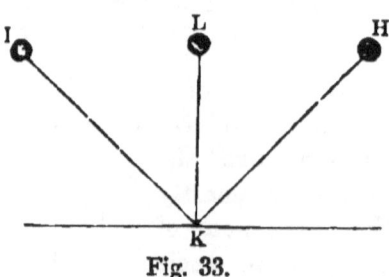

Fig. 33.

209. Thus the two laws of reflexion for perfectly elastic bodies may be stated as follows:

I. **The angles of incidence and reflexion are equal to one another**

II. **The directions of incidence and reflexion lie in the same plane, which also includes a perpendicular drawn to the surface through the point where the body strikes it.**

[A proof of these laws is given in the Appendix, p. 85.]

210. Practical examples of these laws are found in many games. Thus, in the games of fives and racquets, successful play greatly depends upon correctness in mentally judging the angles of incidence and reflexion of the ball, so as to drive it in a direction which makes it difficult for the opposite player to 'return it.' The method of calculating the precise direction in which a ball must be hit in order that, after striking the wall, it may proceed to a given point, is given in the Appendix to this chapter; but of course, in practice, allowance has to be made for the want of perfect elasticity (or 'deadness') of the ball and of the plaster wall of the court.

211. In the game of billiards, both the ivory balls and the india-rubber cushions of the table fulfil much more nearly the conditions of perfect elasticity, and a ball rebounds from the cushion, or from another ball, very nearly indeed in the

theoretical direction. The whole game is full of practical illustrations of the Laws of Motion. In cricket, the position of the surface against which the ball strikes—that is, of the bat, is changed instead of the direction of the ball; and thus when a ball is to be 'sent into the slips,' for instance, the bat is held obliquely, so that the ball strikes it at such an angle as to rebound in the required direction.

APPENDIX A.

212. Proof of the law that when a perfectly elastic body strikes on a perfectly elastic surface, the angle of reflexion is equal to the angle of incidence.

Let AB (fig. 34) represent the direction and magnitude of the force with which the body strikes the surface at B.

Through B draw BC perpendicular to the surface.

Through A draw AD parallel to BC, meeting the surface at D, and AE parallel to the surface, meeting BC in E. Thus AEBD is a parallelogram.

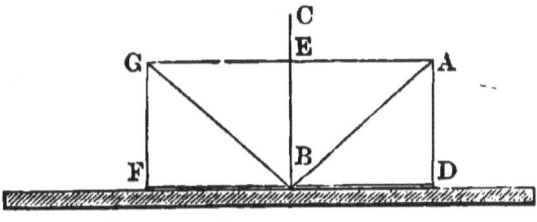

Fig. 34.

Then the force AB may be resolved into two components—namely, DB parallel to the surface, and EB perpendicular to it.

Now, the component DB is not affected by the collision of the ball with the surface; but the component EB is met by an equal and opposite force, or reaction. So that, after the ball has struck the surface, it is acted on by two forces—namely, BF, equal to DB, and BE, equal and opposite to EB.

We have to find the resultant of these forces.

Complete the parallelogram BFGE, and draw the diagonal BG.

Then BG represents the direction and magnitude of the resultant force acting on the ball after it has struck the surface.

It is required to prove that BG makes the same angle with BC that AB does.

Since AE = BD = BF = EG, therefore AE = EG.

And EB is common to the two triangles AEB and GEB.

Also, since AG was drawn parallel to the surface, and BC perpendicular to it, therefore the angle AEB = GEB.

Therefore the triangles AEB and GEB have two sides and one angle equal.

Therefore these triangles are equal.

Therefore the angle GBE is equal to the angle EBA.

Q. E. D.

Appendix B.

213. Problem.—AC and BC, fig. 35, are two of the walls of a fives-court: the ball is at D, and the player wishes to strike it so that, after rebounding from BC, it may hit the point A. In what direction must he hit it?

From D let fall a perpendicular DE upon BC, and produce it to F, making EF = DE.

Join FA, cutting BC in G, and join DG.

Then DG is the direction in which the ball must be hit.

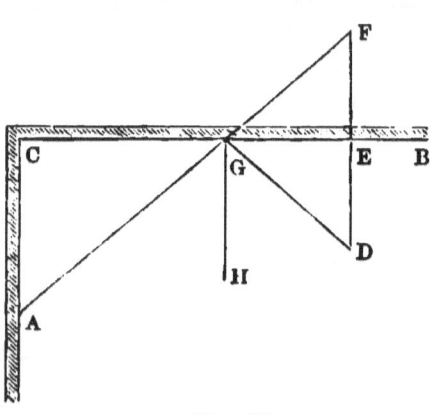

Fig. 35.

Proof.—In the two triangles DEG, FEG, the side DE = EF, and GE is common to the two triangles.

Also the angle DEG = FEG, since both are right angles, DF having been drawn perpendicular to BC.

Therefore these triangles are equal.

Therefore the angle DGE = FGE.

But FGE is equal to the vertically opposite angle CGA; therefore the angle DGE = CGA.

Through G draw GH perpendicular to BC.

Then the angles CGH, HGE are equal, being right angles, and the parts of them, CGA, EGD have been proved equal; therefore the remaining angles, HGA, HGD, are equal.

And these are the angles of incidence and reflexion respectively.

Therefore the ball, if hit in the direction DG, will rebound in the direction GA.

CHAPTER IV.

ACCELERATION.

Section 1.—General Principles.

214. Acceleration means *the quickening of speed caused by the continued action of a force.*

Hitherto the action of forces has, for the most part, been considered as if they acted for an instant only, like the kick given to a football, or the blow of a hammer on a nail. But, strictly speaking, forces seldom do this: their action lasts for an appreciable time, as for instance, the force exerted by gunpowder on a bullet all the time that it is in the barrel of the gun, of an engine in moving a train, of gravitation on a falling stone. Clearly, the longer a force acts on a body, the greater will be the velocity which it imparts to the body; and a little reflection will show that the velocity must be increased in *exact proportion* to the time during which the force acts. Thus, if a force of 1 poundal (par. 158, p. 66) acts continuously for several seconds on a mass of 1 pound, at the end of

1 second, the velocity produced will be 1 foot per second.
2 seconds,   ″   ″   ″   2 feet   ″
3   ″   ″   ″   ″   3   ″   ″
&c. &c.

So that, in order to find out the speed with which a body is moving under the action of a uniform unimpeded force, we have only to multiply the velocity produced in the first second by the number of seconds during which the force has acted.

215. Suppose, for example, that a train is moving out of a station, and that 1 second after the start it is found to be moving at the rate of $1\frac{1}{2}$ feet per second. Then (if it were not for such impediments as the resistance of the air, &c.), at the end of

10 seconds, it will be moving ($10 \times 1\frac{1}{2}$ feet =) 15 feet per second;
20   ″   ″   ($20 \times 1\frac{1}{2}$ feet =) 30   ″   ″

and so on.*

---

* Practically, of course, in the case of a train, the acceleration only goes on up to a certain point, when friction of various kinds just balances the force of the engine. Then there can be no more increase of speed, the whole of the force being expended in overcoming friction, and the continuance of the speed being due to the inertia of the train.

216. The same is true when a force is applied to a moving body in the opposite direction to that in which it is moving; for instance, when a brake is applied to a moving train. If the force applied through the brake is such as would cause a velocity of 5 feet per second, then 5 feet per second will be subtracted from the speed of the train during every second that the brake acts, until the train comes to a stop.

Section 2.—Action of Gravitation.

217. Gravitation is perhaps the best example of a practically uniform accelerating or retarding force at the earth's surface. As already partly explained (p. 30), it makes everything tend to move or 'fall' towards the earth's centre, and it is constantly acting on them while they are doing so. We may now consider more fully what are the results of this continuous accelerating force.

218. We have to find out two things:

1. What is the effect of (a) the material, (b) the mass of a body upon the rate at which it falls?

2. What is the velocity produced in a falling body by gravitation acting on it for 1 second?

Here are questions which cannot be answered by any amount of mere reasoning. We must try experiments, many and varied in character, closely observe the results, and then draw the proper logical inferences from these results. We may accept such deductions as solid scientific truths (until, at any rate, they are disproved by more reliable experiments), whether they agree with our preconceived notions or not.

219. The experiments may be of the following character. (a) Pieces of different materials such as lead, ivory, glass, india-rubber, a fives-ball, &c., but of the *same* weight, may be allowed to fall, starting simultaneously, from a height above the floor; and the order in which they reach the floor may be noted.

[A small box, the bottom of which is hinged like a trap-door, is useful for this experiment. The trap-door should be held by a catch; two or three of the substances mentioned should be put into the box. The latter should then be drawn up to a height above the floor, a box or tray filled with sand being placed on the floor to receive the falling weights, and the catch may be released by a string or a simple electro-magnetic arrangement.]

220. It will be found, as the result of many trials, that all the bodies, whatever they may be made of, if let fall simultaneously from a height, reach the floor at the *same* moment.* And similar experiments made with a large number of substances show that the material of which a body is made has no influence whatever upon the rate of its fall.

221. (*b*) Pieces of the same material, such as lead, but of very different masses (for example, a large bullet and a small one; or a large stone and a piece broken off from it), may be dropped from the box in the manner already described. It will be found that (allowing for the resistance of the air, as explained in the note below) these very different masses of stone or lead reach the floor at the same moment.

222. By such experiments it has been established that the mass of a body has absolutely no influence upon the rate of its fall. This may seem at first sight rather surprising; especially since, if the pieces of lead are lifted, the large piece certainly presses against the hand with greater force than the small piece, and it would appear, therefore, that the former ought to fall quicker. But the result is easily explained if we consider that gravitation has a great deal more work to do in moving the large mass than in moving the small one. Suppose that one body, A, has 10 times as much matter in it as another, B. Then the action of gravitation on A will be 10 times as great as its action on B, but it has 10 times the amount of matter to move, so that it cannot move A any quicker than B.† Thus we may state generally that, the greater the mass of a body is, the greater is the power of gravitation upon it, but the greater also is the

---

* That is, if allowance is made for the fact that, owing to their unequal size, the resistance of the air retards the larger bodies more than the smaller ones; and thus a piece of wood will in its fall lag a little behind a piece of lead of the same weight. In a vacuum the statement is absolutely true.

† As a rough illustration, suppose that a truck drawn by one horse is coupled to another truck of the same weight, also drawn by one horse. Then, though two horses are employed, the trucks will not move any quicker than either separately, because there is twice the weight to move.

work to be done in moving it, so that the body does not fall any quicker.

223. The next point to be considered is—What is the acceleration produced by gravitation in a given time, such as 1 second? The following experiment may be made in order to obtain an answer to this question. Let the box used in the previous experiments, containing a weight such as a brass or ivory ball (the actual weight and material have been shown to have no influence on the result), be drawn up to a height of 16 feet 1 inch above the surface of the sand in the tray below. Let some arrangement for marking seconds, such as a loud-ticking pendulum,* be set working, and let the weight in the box be made to commence its fall at one tick of the pendulum. Then it will be found that the weight reaches the sand just as the second tick sounds. The experiment may be repeated several times to make sure of the result.

224. It will thus be proved that **a body, when allowed to fall freely under the action of gravitation, passes through 16 feet 1 inch in the first second of its fall.**

[In what follows, the distance through which a body falls in 1 second will be considered for simplicity as 16 feet.]

225. From this fact we can deduce the velocity with which it was moving at the end of the second—that is, the acceleration produced by gravitation in 1 second—as follows: The body must, at the end of the second, be moving quicker than 16 feet per second, because it started with no velocity at all, and yet it got through 16 feet in the time. (For example, a runner will do 100 yards in 10 seconds, but at the end of the time he must be running more than 10 yards per second, since he started from rest and moved slowly at first.) In fact, since the acceleration is uniform, at the end of the second it must be moving as much faster than 16 feet per second as it was moving slower than that rate at the beginning of it, thus:

---

* An ordinary metronome may be made to answer; but the best plan is to place the electro-magnet which releases the trap-door in the same circuit as a single-stroke electric bell, and make a seconds pendulum complete the circuit in the middle of its swing.

Velocity at the beginning of the second = 0 ft. per sec.
"   middle   "   " = 16 ft. "
"   end   "   " = 32 ft. "

Since, then, at the end of the second the body must be moving at the rate of 32 feet per second; and since gravitation (for moderately small distances, at any rate) acts uniformly and continuously upon bodies, we may take it as proved that the force of gravitation is one which, at the earth's surface, causes a velocity of 32 feet per second during every second that it acts— that is, that **the acceleration produced by gravitation is 32 feet per second.***

226. We have now ascertained the space fallen through, and the velocity attained by a body at the end of the first second of its fall. A little reflection will enable us to see what space a body will fall through, and what velocity it will have, in succeeding seconds.†

227. The velocity acquired by the body at the end of the first second is 32 feet per second, and if gravitation were to cease at that moment, the body would (by the first Law of Motion) move through 32 feet in the next second. But gravitation goes on acting upon the body, and thus will make it fall another 16 feet in addition to the 32 feet—that is, through $(32 + 16 =)$ 48 feet in all; and also will add another 32 feet per second to its velocity, so that at the end of the second second it will be moving at the rate of $(32 + 32 =)$ 64 feet per second. Similarly, in the third second it will fall through, not merely 64 feet due to its velocity at the beginning of the second, but $(64 + 16 =)$ 80 feet;

---

* The exact value in London is 32 feet 2·3 inches. It varies, as already explained (par. 84, p. 34), with the latitude. The exact acceleration produced by gravitation at the earth's surface in a few latitudes is given below:

Latitude.		Acceleration.	
		ft.	in.
0°	(Equator)	32	1
45°	(Bordeaux)	32	2
51° 30′	(London)	32	2·3
60°	(Stockholm)	32	2·6
90°	(Pole)	32	3

† The spaces and velocities are here so great, that direct experiments on the subject would be difficult to make. But a very ingenious apparatus, called Attwood's machine, has been invented, in which the action of gravitation is so far diluted (as it were) as to bring it within reasonable bounds.

and it will at the end of the second have a velocity of (64 + 32 =) 96 feet per second. By the same course of reasoning, we can calculate its progress during succeeding seconds.

228. In order to find the total space fallen through in a given number of seconds, we have only to add together the spaces fallen through in each second. Thus the total distance through which a stone falls in two seconds is 16 feet + 48 feet, or 64 feet.

The following table will show the results already arrived at:

Time of fall.	Velocity at end of time.	Space fallen through in the second.	Total space fallen through.
1 second,	32 ft. per sec.	16 feet.	16 feet.
2 seconds,	64 "	48 "	64 "
3 "	96 "	80 "	144 "
4 "	128 "	112 "	256 "
5 "	160 "	144 "	400 "

229. From the above table it is easy to see that there is a very simple relation between the time of fall and the total space passed through in the time. Thus:

In 1 second the space passed through is 16 feet.
In 2 seconds   "   "   64 " = 16 × 4 (or 2^2).
In 3   "   "   "   144 " = 16 × 9 (or 3^2).
In 4   "   "   "   256 " = 16 × 16 (or 4^2).

That is, the total space fallen through increases with the *square of the time of fall*. Thus we get the following simple rule for finding how far a body will fall in a given time:

Take the square of the number of seconds, and multiply 16 feet by it; the product is the distance fallen through.

For example: A bag of sand was let fall from a balloon, and reached the ground in 8 seconds. The square of 8 is 64; and 16 × 64 = 1024 feet. Hence the distance of the balloon from the earth was 1024 feet.

230. The above example illustrates a practical application of the laws of gravitation which have been explained—namely, a method for finding approximately the height of a tower or cliff, or the depth of a well. We have only to let a stone drop, and observe accurately how many seconds elapse before it touches

the ground (or the water in a well), and then apply the above rule. Thus, if a stone dropped from the top of a cliff took 5 seconds to reach the base, then $5^2 = 25$, and $16 \times 25 = 400$; thus the cliff was 400 feet high. It would really be rather less than this, since the resistance of the air checks the speed of the falling stone, so that in the 5 seconds it really fell less than 400 feet.

231. The acceleration produced by gravitation explains why hailstones do so much damage although they are so small. They have fallen from a great height, and thus have acquired a very high velocity; hence their momentum is considerable in spite of their small mass. We also see why, when water falls from a height, as in a waterfall, it breaks into drops before it has gone far. The lower part of the descending mass of water has a much higher speed than the upper part, because it has been falling longer; hence it breaks off from the rest, and separates into drops, which separate more and more as they descend. When a viscid liquid, like treacle, is poured out from a height, the bulky sluggish stream becomes gradually rapid and smaller, and is at last reduced to a thread; but wherever a vessel is held into the stream, it fills equally fast.

232. We may next consider what happens when a body such as a cricket-ball is thrown straight up into the air. At the moment it leaves the hand it has a certain velocity, and if nothing occurred to stop it, it would (according to the first Law of Motion) go on rising continually with undiminished speed. But gravitation acts upon it quite irrespectively of any motion it may have from the action of other forces (according to the second Law of Motion), and, by pulling it downwards, gradually lessens its upward motion until it comes to rest. But it does not stop there; gravitation is still acting on it, and it begins to fall with accelerated motion in the usual way. Now, it is pretty easy to see that, since gravitation acts upon it through the same space during its fall as during its rise, the force will produce in the ball the same velocity, by the time it reaches its starting-point, as it had when it originally started. For example, suppose that the action of gravitation stopped its upward motion in 3 seconds. Then since we know (see table in par. 228) that gravitation is a force capable of producing in

3 seconds a velocity of 96 feet per second, and since the force required to destroy a given motion must be equal to the force which has produced that motion, therefore the ball, when it left the hand, must have been moving at the rate of 96 feet per second, and when it returns to its starting-point, will have the same velocity.

233. Hence it follows:

(1) That a body thrown or shot upwards takes just as long to fall as it does to rise.

(2) That the height to which it rises is equal to the space through which it would fall by gravitation in the observed time of its rise. Thus, if the body is 3 seconds in the air before it stops rising, it must (see table, p. 92) have risen to a height of 144 feet.

(3) That the force with which it strikes any obstacle placed at the same level as its starting-point (such as a hand held out to catch it), is equal to the force which was originally used to propel it upwards.

234. We thus learn:

(1) How to calculate approximately the height to which a ball or arrow, projected upwards, has ascended. We have only to observe the number of seconds which elapse between the moment of its start and the moment it returns to its starting-point again. Half of this time will have been spent in falling, and we can calculate, by the rule already given (p. 92), what space it must have fallen through in the known time. This space must, of course, be equal to the height to which it has risen. Thus, supposing that an arrow shot upwards takes 12 seconds to return to the level of its starting-point. It will have occupied 6 seconds in falling, and therefore must have passed through ($6^2 \times 16 =$) 576 feet. Hence it must have risen to a height of 576 feet.

235. This has been practically applied to determine the height to which stones shot upwards from volcanoes have ascended. In a recent eruption of Vesuvius, rocks were projected out of the crater, which were observed to be 10 seconds in the air before falling into the crater again. These rocks must have been 5 seconds in falling, and hence they must have risen to a height of ($5^2 \times 16 =$) 400 feet.

(2) The reason why it is so dangerous to hit racquet-balls away at random, and fire bullets up into the air. The force with which such a ball hits any object in its fall is equal to the force with which it was originally projected upwards (excepting, of course, the loss due to resistance of the air); and several fatal accidents have happened from this cause.

CHAPTER V.
CENTRE OF GRAVITY.
Section 1.—General Principles.

236. In examining the laws of falling bodies, we have simply considered the earth, as a whole, to attract a body, as a whole, towards itself. But every body is made up of a very large number of molecules, and the force of gravitation acts between each separate molecule and every other one. In the case of a solid, the molecules, being fast bound together by the force of cohesion, must necessarily move all together, like well-drilled soldiers, when they move at all; and we do not notice the separate attractions of the individual molecules. But in fact each molecule of a falling stone is being pulled sideways, right and left, as well as downwards, by the earth's molecules, as indicated in fig. 36. Now, on the principle of the Composition of Forces already explained (p. 68), all these separate forces can be shown to be equivalent to one resultant force acting between a certain point in the earth and a certain point in the stone; and these points are called the **centres of gravity** of the earth and the stone respectively.

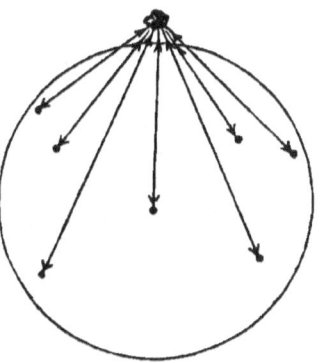

Fig. 36.

The centre of gravity of a body, then, may be defined as **the place where the resultant of all the attracting forces** between the separate molecules of the body is considered to be applied.*

237. It follows from this that, if we want to support any solid body—that is, to counteract the effect of gravitation in making it fall—we need not put props under every part of it (though the earth is attracting every part), but only one prop at the centre of gravity, or else *directly above* or *directly below* the centre of gravity; because one force applied there in the opposite direction will counteract the resultant of all the earth's forces. Thus one man can carry a long ladder on one of his shoulders, and a ruler or a stick of uniform thickness may be poised on the tip of one finger, if supported just at its middle point, where (as will be shown, p. 106) the centre of gravity lies.

Section 2.—Equilibrium of Bodies.

238. When anything rests on a support without showing a tendency to move of its own accord, it is said to be **in equilibrium** (Lat. *æquus*, equal; *librare*, to balance); because the attraction of gravitation on any one part of the body, tending to pull that part downwards, is balanced by an equal attraction on some other part of the body on the opposite side of the support, so that the body has no tendency to tumble off its support in one direction more than another.

239. It is a matter of common experience that most bodies will rest much more steadily in some positions than in others: a book, for instance, rests on a table much more steadily when laid on its side than when standing on its edge; an egg, when placed on its side, will remain in that position, but we find great difficulty in balancing it on either end. It is important, then, to examine what are the true conditions of equilibrium, and

---

* It must be noted that the point we call the 'centre of gravity' of a body is not in all cases in the same position. The direction in which a stone falls at any particular place on the earth's surface passes through a point in the earth which is the 'centre of gravity' for bodies at that place: but the directions in which things fall at other places do not, as a rule, pass through precisely the same point, although the variation is small and may usually be neglected. In fact, comparatively few bodies have (like spheres) a 'centre' of gravity (as defined in the text) which is invariable in position under all conditions.

a few simple experiments of the following kind may be made to illustrate them.

Take a flat circular piece of wood, about six or eight inches in diameter and half an inch thick,* and bore holes in different parts of it, such as *a, b, c, d*, fig. 37; one of these, *a*, being in the exact centre, which is (as will be presently shown) the position of the centre of gravity. Support a piece of thick wire (a small pencil, or the thin end of a penholder, will do) horizontally, and hang the board on it, trying the various holes in succession, and noting carefully under what conditions the board remains in equilibrium, and when it rests most steadily and least steadily on the support.

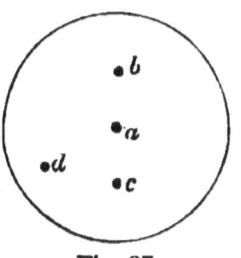

Fig. 37.

240. It will be found:

(1) That the board will only remain in equilibrium—that is, without moving when the hand is taken away—when the support is either *at* the centre of gravity, or directly *above* the centre of gravity, or else directly *below* the centre of gravity. A plumb-line (fig. 4, p. 30) should be held close to the board in order to define the exact positions called 'above' and 'below' (see p. 31).

(2) That when the support is at the centre of gravity, the board will rest in any position indifferently, and will require very little force to move it from one position to another.

(3) That the board rests much more steadily when the point of support is *above* the centre of gravity than when it is below the centre of gravity; so much so that, if the board is pushed away from this position, it tends to come back thither of its own accord; whereas, if the support is *below* the centre of gravity, there is some little difficulty in placing the board in equilibrium at all, and a very slight touch makes it leave this position and swing round until it finally settles in such a position that the centre of gravity is as low as it can get.

241. These facts show that the steadiness of anything depends upon where the support is placed with reference to the centre

---

* A piece of very thick cardboard will answer, but not so well.

of gravity, and whether the centre of gravity is likely to be *raised* or *lowered* when the body is put into some other position. Thus we are able to distinguish three different kinds of equilibrium, called **stable, neutral,** and **unstable equilibrium** respectively.

(1) **Stable equilibrium.**

242. This is when the body rests steadily and requires some force to move it; and, when it is moved, it tries to get back to its former position.

Examples of bodies in stable equilibrium are—a table or chair, a book lying flat on the table, a man standing on both feet.

In this kind of equilibrium the support is so placed that the centre of gravity would be *raised* by altering the position of the body. Thus, if the book be raised from its flat position, turning on one of its edges as if on a hinge, it is evident that its centre of gravity (which is nearly its middle point) will be raised higher than it was before.

(2) **Unstable equilibrium.**

243. This is when the body is easily moved, and if moved a little way, tends to go on moving farther from its original position until the centre of gravity is as low as it can get. That is, the body is 'top-heavy,' or tends to overturn.

As examples of this may be taken—a chair balanced on one leg, a top balanced on its point, a cricket-bat standing on its handle, a man walking on stilts.

In this case, the support is so placed that the centre of gravity would get lower when the body is moved from its position. If, for instance, the cricket-bat resting on its handle was pushed sideways, its centre of gravity (which is not far from the centre of the blade) would get lower and lower until it lay flat on the ground.

(3) **Neutral equilibrium.**

244. This is when the body is easily moved, but will rest in *any* position indifferently.

For example, a carriage wheel whether supported at its centre or at its edge, a roller, a cricket-ball, resting on a horizontal surface.

In this case the support is so placed that the centre of gravity is not raised or lowered by altering the position of the body. In a wheel, for instance, the centre of gravity of which is at its centre, this point is not raised or lowered when it turns on an axle; and if it rolls along a horizontal road, the centre of gravity remains at the same height above the road (since all radii of a circle are equal), and the point where the wheel is supported by the road is always vertically below the centre of gravity.

245. Many bodies can, from their shape, be supported in such positions as to illustrate all the three kinds of equilibrium. Thus, a cone, fig. 38, when resting on its base a, is in **stable equilibrium**, since,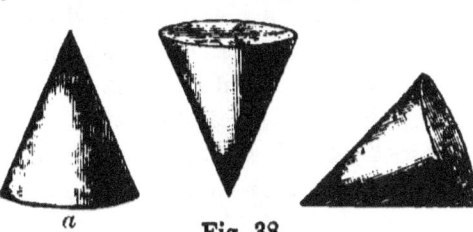

Fig. 38.

if it is tilted on any part of its edge in order to push it over, the

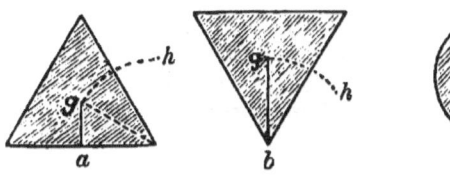

Fig. 39.

centre of gravity is raised, passing along the curve $g\,h$, fig. 39, and this is resisted at first by the whole effect of the weight of the body. When placed on its point, as shown in b, it is in **unstable equilibrium**, since the slightest lateral push causes the centre of gravity to move along the descending curve shown in the figure, and thus a portion of the weight of the body aids in pulling it over. When the cone is laid on its side, as shown in c, it is in **neutral equilibrium**, and will remain in any position on a horizontal surface, since the centre of gravity cannot be made higher or lower by moving the body over the surface, as explained with reference to the carriage wheel. An egg, when resting on its side, is in **stable equilibrium** or in **neutral equilibrium**, according to the direction in which it is moved; when resting on its end, it is in **unstable equilibrium**. The reason will be sufficiently obvious from what has been already said.

General Laws of Equilibrium.

Law I.—A body is in stable equilibrium as long as a perpendicular line drawn through the centre of gravity falls some way within the base on which it rests.

246. The following experiment will illustrate the truth of this law. Take a block of wood about the size and shape of a brick (or a brick itself will do), and drive a small nail into the exact centre of one of its sides (which, as will be shortly proved, defines the position of the centre of gravity of the block). Place the block on one end at the edge of a table, and hang from the nail a small plumb-line, long enough to reach a little way below the edge of the table, fig. 40. Apply pressure near the top of

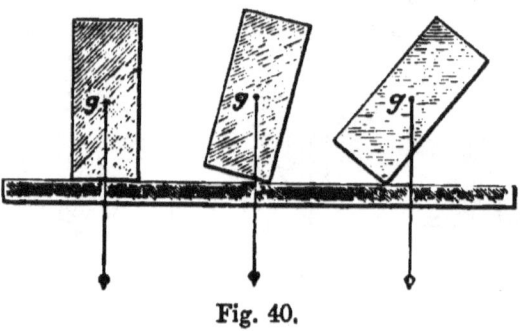

Fig. 40.

the block so as to tilt it a little way on one of its edges. Considerable force will be required at first to move it, and it will come back again to its former steady position when the pressure is removed. It is, in fact, in stable equilibrium. Now tilt it farther by degrees, noting the position of the plumb-line with regard to the edge on which the block is being tilted. The line will gradually approach this edge; but so long as it is well within the edge, the block will show stable equilibrium, although less and less force will be required to move it. As soon as it is tilted so far that the line passes in the least degree beyond the edge of the base, the block will go on moving in the same direction, and will topple over. The same result will be obtained if the block is similarly tilted on the other edge.

247. The reason of the law is easily seen. As long as a

perpendicular line (defined by the plumb-line) falls within the base on which a body rests, some part of the support is vertically below the centre of gravity: and this, as has been shown in par. 237, p. 96, is all that is necessary to keep the whole mass up. Moreover, if we observe the curve described by the centre of gravity as the body is tilted on one edge (as if on a hinge or axis), it will be seen to be an ascending curve, as in the case of the cone, fig. 39, *a.* Hence the centre of gravity must be raised when the body is thus tilted, and force enough to overcome nearly its whole weight must be at first applied.

248. Thus we see that the farther a perpendicular drawn through the centre of gravity lies within the base, the more stable is the equilibrium of the body. A pyramidal or conical building is the steadiest and firmest of structures, because the base is so large and the centre of gravity so low that the latter would have to be raised almost vertically upwards by any force tending to overthrow the structure, and a considerable change of position would be required before a perpendicular drawn through the centre of gravity would reach the edge of the base. The legs of a table or a tripod are often spread outwards, so as to increase the size of the base. A wall, tower, or chimney stands steadiest when quite upright, and masons take great pains to insure perfect uprightness of the building by constant use of the plumb-line.

249. A tower may, however, lean some way from the perpendicular, and overhang its base, without actually falling, although its stability is lessened, as already shown. Such an inclination is sometimes produced by the foundations giving way on one side, and the precise extent to which it may proceed without rendering the building actually unsafe may be calculated on the principles already explained. The most famous example is the Leaning Tower of Pisa in North Italy (fig. 41, next page), which is 180 feet high and 52 feet in diameter. It leans so far that a plumb-line let down from the top touches the ground 14 feet from the base of the building; but it might, as can easily be proved, lean more than twice as much without actually toppling over.

250. A man stands firmly when resting upright on both feet, and his steadiness is increased by placing the feet wide apart as

sailors do. In resting on one foot, the centre of gravity of the body must be thrown over that foot; hence, in walking, the body is almost unconsciously swayed slightly from side to side. The fact is forced into notice when two men walk close together, but do not keep step; one putting forward his right foot and the

Fig. 41.—Leaning Tower of Pisa.

other his left foot at the same moment. They then jostle each other, one leaning to the right and the other to the left at the same time.

251. In dancing, walking on stilts, and skating, we have examples of still more refined series of experiments on keeping the centre of gravity over the base, or 'preserving one's balance,' as it is commonly called. The narrower the base, such as the end of a stilt or the edge of a skate, the less is the lateral movement required to throw the perpendicular drawn through the centre of gravity outside it—that is, the more unstable is the equilibrium.* A performer on the tight rope holds a long pole

* In skating, the principles of inertia and centrifugal tendency (Chapter III., Sect. 2) are called in to aid us. Forward progress on the edge of the skate is made in a series of curves, the skater not caring always to keep his centre of

horizontally, and when in his movements the perpendicular through his centre of gravity falls outside the rope, he brings it back again by quickly shifting the pole a little to the opposite side.

Law II.—**The lower the centre of gravity is, the more stable is the equilibrium of the body.**

252. The truth of this law may be shown by the following method. Take a flat wooden rod, about 12 inches long, 2 inches broad, and $\frac{1}{2}$ inch thick, fitted with a leaden weight which is capable of sliding along it, but clasps it so tightly as to remain in any required position, fig. 42. Bore a hole through the centre of the piece of wood, and hang it on a horizontal wire or small peg. Adjust the sliding weight until the rod will remain indifferently in any position. Then it is in neutral equilibrium, and we know that the centre of gravity must be at the point of support. Slide the weight a short way along the rod; the latter will now take a position of stable equilibrium, in which the centre of gravity is below the support; but a very slight pressure will be sufficient to move it on one side, and it will swing backwards and forwards slowly until it regains its first position. Next lower the weight, and therefore also the centre of gravity, still farther: the rod will now require a greater pressure to move it, and after a few quick swings it will settle decidedly into its original position. If, finally, the weight is put quite close to the end of the rod, the equilibrium will be found to be still more stable.

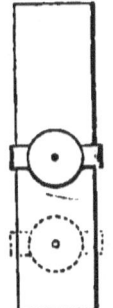

Fig. 42.

253. The reason of the law is plain: for the lower the centre of gravity is already, the more likely it is to be raised by any change in the position of the body. Moreover, if the body is supported on a broad base, and the centre of gravity is low (as in fig. 39 a), any change in the position of the body effected by tilting it on one edge of its base must raise the centre of gravity nearly vertically upwards, and this is resisted by the whole

gravity directly over his skate, but preserving himself from falling by balancing his centrifugal tendency against gravitation. The theory of the use of the bicycle is of a very similar character.

weight of the body. Even when the base is narrow, it is easy to see that the centre of gravity, when it is low down, has to be moved through a *greater* distance and along a *more sharply-ascending* curve before a perpendicular through it falls outside the base, than when it is high up in the body.

254. A cart loaded with hay is, when tilted by one wheel passing over a heap of stones, as in fig. 43, much more likely to upset than when loaded with the same weight of stones or iron. For the load of stones would only fill the cart up to the top of the sideboards, so that its centre of gravity would be near C, and a perpendicular drawn through it would still fall a little within the wheelbase; but the load of hay would be piled up much higher, and the centre of gravity would be near C′, the perpendicular through which would fall outside the wheel. Similarly, a coach with luggage packed low is much less likely to be overturned than when passengers and luggage are on the top.

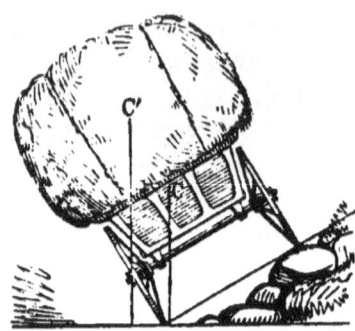

Fig. 43.

255. The safety of a ship depends on many tons of 'ballast' being put as low as possible in the hold, so that when the ship rolls in a heavy sea, the centre of gravity may always be raised, and then in its descent it will tend to bring the whole mass back to an upright position. A boat is more liable to upset if passengers stand up in it, because the centre of gravity is raised so high that the whole may be put into unstable equilibrium. The same principle explains why there is so much risk in tossing oars in a light boat, and why it is so difficult at first to manage an outrigged boat, although when the oars are tied into the rowlocks a much broader base is gained while they rest on or in the water.

256. A cone may be made to rest steadily on its point by fixing weights to it below, as shown in fig. 44, because the centre of gravity of the whole mass (cone and weights) can be thus brought down below the point of support. A coin may in a similar way be balanced on the point of a needle, by being

affixed to a cork on each side of which is stuck a fork or a

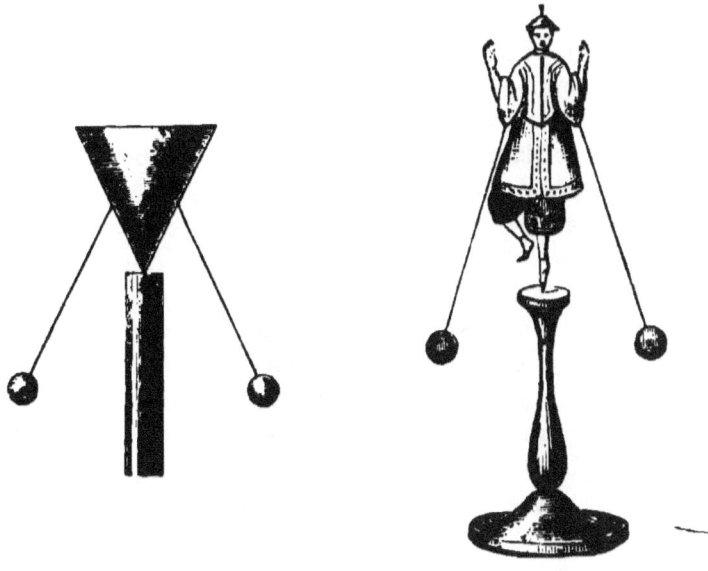

Fig. 44. Fig. 45.

pocket-knife sloping downwards. Many toys are constructed on a similar principle, one of which is shown in fig. 45.

General Illustrations of the Laws of Equilibrium.

257. Only a few of these can be mentioned here; many others will suggest themselves to those who think over the subject.

(1) The necessity for balancing the parts of quickly-moving machinery. If, for instance, a wheel is heavier in one part than another, its centre of gravity will not coincide with the centre on which it turns, and will therefore be swaying from side to side at each revolution; thus from the inertia of the mass and its reaction against the force which swings it, the whole framework is made to vibrate and strained.

(2) The method of setting a swing in motion. This depends upon quick changes in position, so made as to shift the centre of gravity from one side of the vertical position of the swing to the other; this sets up a swinging motion which is increased by properly timed movements of the same kind.

(3) The reason why an umbrella, or a cricket-bat, is more

easily balanced on its heaviest end. The centre of gravity in this case is comparatively low down, and only moves through a *small* distance round the point of support while the whole object sways through a considerable arc, so that the supporting finger is more easily by a slight movement kept exactly below the centre of gravity.

258. It will be useful to think over and explain, on the principles above given, such simple problems as the reasons why it would be unsafe to add much to the height of, or to hang a set of heavy bells near the top of the leaning tower of Pisa—why a candlestick is more liable to upset when a long candle is in it than when the candle has burned down to the socket—why a man with a load on his back leans forward; if he is carrying a box in one hand he leans to the opposite side—why a man standing against a wall cannot stoop forward to pick up anything while both his heels are against the wall—why if his side touches the wall he cannot lift the outside foot from the ground without falling—why he leans forward in rising from a chair.

SECTION 3.—METHODS OF FINDING THE CENTRE OF GRAVITY.

259. In cases where the body is uniform in structure throughout, and symmetrical in shape, the centre of gravity can be found by simple measurement; since all that we have to do is to find its exact middle point round which all the molecules are regularly arranged, so that there are just as many of them on one side of this point as on the other.

(1) To find the centre of gravity of a very thin straight rod, which is uniform—that is, alike in every part.

Rule.—**Find the exact middle point of its length: the centre of gravity will be at this point.**

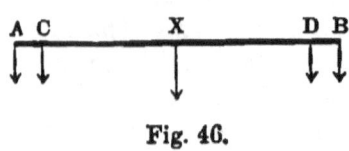

Fig. 46.

This may be proved as follows: The resultant of the forces exerted by gravitation on the two end-molecules A and B, fig. 46, must be midway between them—that is, at X. The resultant of the forces on the next two, C and D, must be also midway between them—that is, at X; and so on for the rest. Therefore the resultant of all the attractions will be at the middle point, X, of the rod; and this will be the centre of gravity.

260. To illustrate this, a thin straight piece of steel wire, about 16 or 18 inches long, may be taken, and its exact middle point found by measurement, and marked. If it is hung up by a piece of string tied to it just at this point, it will be found to balance horizontally; which could only occur if the centre of gravity was just where the support is.*

(2) To find the centre of gravity of a thin uniform plate, shaped like a parallelogram.

Rule.—**Find the middle point of its length, and through this point draw a line across the plate parallel to the ends. Find also the middle point of its breadth, and through this point draw a line along the plate parallel to its sides.**

Then the point where these lines cross will be the centre of gravity of the plate.

Proof of this: The plate may be regarded as made up of a number of thin rods side by side, such as AB, CD, &c., fig. 47; and the centre of gravity of each of these will be in the middle of its length. Therefore the centre of gravity of the whole will be somewhere along the line WX.

Similarly, the plate may be considered to be made up of a number of rods EF, GH, &c., fig. 48; and the centre of gravity

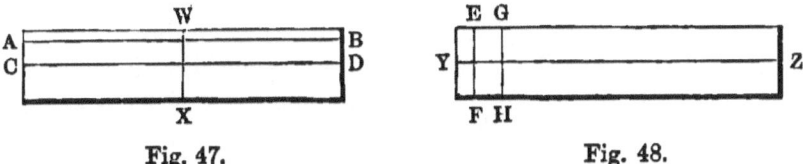

Fig. 47.   Fig. 48.

of each of these will be in the middle of its length; so that the centre of gravity of the whole must be somewhere along the line YZ.

And since it has already been proved to be in the line WX, it must be at the point where these two lines cross.

261. To prove this experimentally, take a piece of thick card-

---

* Strictly speaking, it should balance in any position; but the stiffness of the string prevents this.

board, about 12 inches long, and 2 inches broad, and draw on it the lines as above directed: bore a hole (best with a sharp leather-punch) exactly at the point where the lines intersect, pass a piece of string through the hole, and bring it up on each side of the cardboard, so as to suspend the latter in a wide loop. If the work has been carefully done, the cardboard will hang in neutral equilibrium, showing that the centre of gravity is where the support is. Also the cardboard may be hung by a piece of string passed through the hole and knotted below: it will be found to hang horizontally.

262. It should be observed that in the above cases what has really been found is the centre of gravity of the surface-layer. If the rod or plate is very thin, this will be nearly the true centre of gravity of the whole mass: but if it has a sensible thickness, the centre of gravity will be midway between the centres of gravity of its two surfaces.

263. On the same principle—namely, by regarding the body as made up of a number of thin rods—the centre of gravity of any regularly-shaped body may be proved to lie at the exact centre of its figure. For example, the position of the centre of gravity of a round disc, such as a wheel; of a cylinder, such as a round ruler; and of a sphere, such as a cricket-ball, is known exactly; although we cannot always practically get at it.

264. The position of the centre of gravity of a triangular-shaped plate is not quite so obvious, but it may readily be found by the following rule: Bisect any two of the sides of the triangle, and draw lines from the points thus found, D, E, fig. 49, to the opposite angles at A and C. The centre of gravity lies at the point where these lines cross, F.

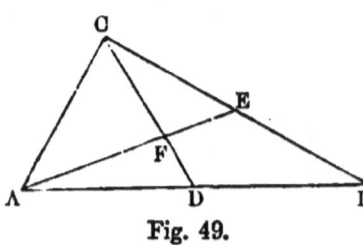

Fig. 49.

The truth of this rule depends on the same principle as that above explained: the small rods being supposed to diminish gradually in length up to a point of the triangle. It may be useful to remember that (as can be easily proved from Euclid) the centre of gravity of a triangle is one-third of the way up from the base to the apex.

Method of finding the Centre of Gravity by Experiment.

265. This method is applicable to all bodies, even though their shape is irregular and their density unequal in different parts. The principle of it is this—that when anything, supported at one point, is in stable equilibrium, the centre of gravity must be somewhere along a perpendicular line drawn through, or let fall from, the point of support (as has been already shown in par. 246, p. 100).

266. The experiment is performed thus:

(1) Hang the thing up by a point near the edge, and let it take up a position of stable equilibrium.

(2) Hang a plumb-line from the same point, and mark the direction of the perpendicular line on the body. Then the centre of gravity must be somewhere along this line.

(3) Hang the object up by another point, and mark the perpendicular line through this point, in the same way as before. Then the centre of gravity must be in this line, as well as the first line.

Therefore it must be where the two lines cross.

267. In illustration of the method, take an irregular piece of cardboard, fig. 50, bore a hole near the edge at any part, as at A (the hole must not be so large as shown in the figure), and hang it on a horizontal pin. Hang a heavy plumb-line from the same pin, and mark with a pencil the lowest point, B, where the line is over the cardboard (the two should hang just clear of each other); then remove the plumb-line, and draw a straight line from the centre of the hole to the point just marked. Bore a hole in another part of the cardboard, as at C, and mark the direction of the

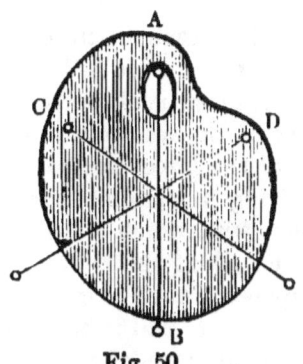

Fig. 50.

perpendicular in the same way. To insure accuracy, it will be as well to bore a third hole, as at D, and mark the perpendicular through it as before. If proper care has been taken, all the three perpendiculars should cross in the same point; and the centre of gravity may be proved to lie at this point by hanging the card from this point by a string, and observing that it is in a condition of neutral equilibrium.

268. The centre of gravity of many bodies does not lie in the substance of the body itself, but in the space outside its surface. Thus the centre of gravity of a chair, as determined by the method above described, see fig. 51, is in the space below the seat; and the centre of gravity of a ring is in the centre of the space within the circle of the ring.

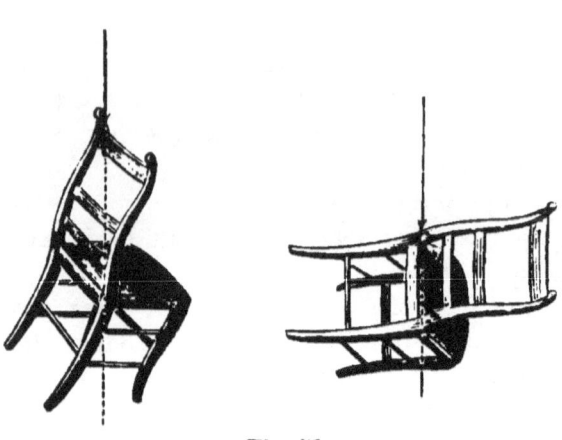

Fig. 51.

APPENDIX.

Centre of Percussion, or of Inertia.

269. Although, in considering the point called the centre of gravity, we have hitherto referred to the force of gravitation only, yet it must be observed that the same point is the point of application of the resultant of *any* set of parallel forces acting on the body, or of the force exerted by the body itself when its molecules are all moving in parallel lines at the same rate, as one mass. Thus the force with which a cricket-ball strikes the bat acts as if it was all collected at the centre of gravity of the ball. But it must not be supposed that the centre of gravity of the bat is the proper place to strike the ball; because, as the bat is swung in the hand, the different parts of it are not moving at the same rate, those farther from the hand moving quicker and therefore having more momentum than those nearer to it. There is, however, a point in the bat which has a momentum which is the *average* of the momenta of all the different parts, and this is the point where the ball ought to be struck. It is called the **centre of percussion** or **centre of inertia**; and when the ball is struck there, the bat acts as if all the

force applied to it was concentrated at the point in the direction in which the ball is to be hit, and the bat 'drives' well. If the ball is not struck by this point, the reaction of it tends to turn the whole bat round on the true centre of percussion as if on a pivot, and the hand is jarred (the bat 'stings,' as the expression is), so that sometimes the bat is lost hold of. The centre of percussion is nearer to the end of a bat than the centre of gravity; in a stick of uniform thickness (like that used for 'rounders') it is, when the stick is swung round one end as a pivot, one-third of the whole length from the outer end, as may be proved by hitting a rail with the stick, and noting when least vibration is felt by the hand.

CHAPTER VI.
ENERGY AND WORK.
SECTION 1.—GENERAL PRINCIPLES.

270. When we say of a man that he 'has energy,' we mean that he shows great power of overcoming difficulties, that he is an active man of business, that he is capable of doing, and ready to do, a large amount of work. Similarly in natural science, when we observe a body, such as a moving cannon-ball, to be capable of doing mechanical work, such as knocking down a wall or piercing a hole through an iron plate, we say that there is 'energy' in it.

271. **Work** means the overcoming of obstacles, such as the setting a body in motion against the resistance which inertia, cohesion, &c. oppose to motion. For example, the cannon-ball does work when it knocks aside the heavy stones of the wall, or drives before it the molecules of the iron armour-plate in spite of the toughness of the material. A locomotive engine does work when it overcomes the inertia of the train and forces its way through the resisting air. Energy, then, may be defined as **the condition of a body which makes it capable of doing work.**

272. We have already spoken of a moving cannon-ball as having momentum (p. 41), which was explained to mean the force with which it is moving; but practically we are much more closely concerned with the work which such a cannon-ball will do before its motion is stopped, than with speculations on

the supposed force which is in it during its flight; and it is satisfactory to be able to turn from the rather shadowy conception of 'quantity of motion,' and consider the actual tangible results in the shape of work which can be got out of a body having energy in it.

273. In the first place, it is found that work can only be done while energy is being transferred from one piece of matter to another. A cannon-ball does no work while it is moving through the air (except the comparatively slight amount done in knocking aside the particles of air in its way); it is only when it comes to something which can and will take some of the energy out of it—some resistance, in fact—that we observe work to be done. Then energy passes out of the ball into the particles of stone or iron which it displaces (the splinters would, if collected, do as much damage as the ball*), and the ball itself comes to rest, having lost the energy which was imparted to it in the gun. Similarly, a moving billiard-ball loses little energy in travelling over the table, but when it strikes against another ball, its energy is transferred to that ball, which immediately moves on at the same rate (as we have seen, p. 82) as the first ball, while the latter stops dead owing to loss of its energy,† and can do no more work until struck by the cue.

Section 2.—Statical and Kinetic Energy.

274. In the next place it is observable that a body may have a great deal of energy in it even though it is not moving at all.‡ An energetic man is not always displaying his energy by doing work, although he may 'have it in him' (as the phrase is). Similarly, there may be a great deal of mechanical energy stored up in a body ready for transfer and work, but giving no

---

* Except, of course, that some of the energy passes into the form of heat.

† It may be noticed that this may possibly indicate a simple explanation of the fact of an action being always met by a reaction (as stated in Law III., p. 77). The truth is, not that there is any real force developed anew in the reaction, but that the moving body, after striking another body, has less energy by precisely the amount which it gave up in striking that other body, and therefore is so much the less capable of moving on against resistance. Thus exactly the same effect in lessening or stopping its motion is produced, as if an equivalent of new force had been applied in the opposite direction to the body.

‡ Observe the distinction here between momentum and energy. A body can only have momentum when it is moving; it may have energy when motionless.

sign of its presence. For example, place an iron 1 lb. weight upon a piece of glass laid on the table. The weight presses on the glass, but has not energy enough to break it. Now raise the weight, and hang it by a piece of string about 2 feet above the glass. The weight now, although motionless, has more energy in it than before; as may be proved by cutting the string, when the weight will do the work of breaking the glass to pieces, which it could not do before. The energy in a body which is not actually doing work is called **Statical Energy** ($\sigma\tau\alpha\tau\iota\varkappa\grave{o}\varsigma$, 'at rest'), or sometimes **Potential Energy** (*potentia*, power). On the other hand, energy while in the act of being transferred and doing work is called **Kinetic Energy** ($\varkappa\iota\nu\eta\tau\iota\varkappa\grave{o}\varsigma$, 'fit for causing motion').

275. In illustration, we may trace the changes of energy in the weight of a clock. While it is being wound up, it gains energy, which is put into it as kinetic energy by the muscular power which raises it against the attraction of gravitation. Before it begins to fall, this energy remains as **statical energy**, depending on the position of the weight as raised above the floor. While it is falling, it gives out the energy as **kinetic energy** in turning the wheels of the clock. When it has reached the point from which it was raised, all the energy which it had gained in being wound up is spent; and if it can fall no farther, no more work can be got out of it. So also in a watch, when the spring is coiled up, energy is transferred to it from the muscles of the hand which winds it, and this is stored up in it as **statical energy**, and given out gradually as **kinetic energy** in making the watch go.* When a train is going up an incline, some of the power of the steam is being stored up as **statical energy**, which carries the train down the next incline without much help from the engine. Water in a river or lake at a higher level than the sea possesses **statical energy**, which it gives out while falling to the sea-level, as **kinetic energy** in turning the water-wheels of mills, carrying boats down stream, &c.

---

* Thus we are in fact ourselves working our own watches and clocks; storing up at intervals in the powerless machinery sufficient statical energy to keep it moving, while being gradually given out as kinetic energy, for a day or a week without further supply.

276. Let us consider what happens to the water when it has got down to the sea-level. Gravitation can move it no farther, and (like a clock weight which has run down) it can do no more useful work. But the heat of the sun now supplies it with energy enough to enable it to rise in the form of vapour, against the force of gravitation, high in the air above the earth's surface. There, as it loses heat, it condenses into mist or cloud, and then begins its downward course as drops of rain. Some of it falls into the sea again, but much of it falls on hills and high levels, and collects in streams and lakes, from which its course was traced above.

277. It is worth especial notice how very much of the work done on the earth is due to energy supplied by the sun. All the power gained from water is, as we have just seen, due to this cause. Winds also, which work mills and propel ships, are simply currents of air caused by the sun's heat. But steam is now extensively used instead of wind or water power for driving mills, &c. Now, the energy of the steam which drives the engine is put into it by the heat produced by the coal burnt under the boiler. This coal is the remains of trees and plants which grew on the earth many ages ago, and the energy necessary for their growth was supplied to them by the sun's rays, and these only. As long as plants are in light they flourish, and no longer.* Therefore the work done by our modern engines is due to the sun's energy stored up in a statical form on the earth in very early times.

278. So again with regard to the living machine of the human body. We gain the power of doing work from the food we eat, as any one may prove by trying to play cricket, or row, or run, or read, without breakfast or dinner. Now, our food is partly vegetable, such as bread, tea, potatoes; partly animal, such as meat, milk, butter. The corn, potatoes, &c. derive their power of growth from the sun, as has just been explained. The animals whose flesh, &c. we use as food, live and

---

* What actually happens is this: Plants feed upon carbon dioxide ('carbonic acid'), a compound of carbon and oxygen which exists in air. While light falls upon them, they have the power of decomposing this substance, combining with its carbon, and giving out its oxygen to the air. When they are burnt, their carbon combines again with oxygen, and in doing this a great deal of energy is made available in the form of heat.

thrive on grass and other plants, which themselves live by the sun.

279. Thus the sun is really working our trains, grinding as well as growing our corn, weaving our clothes, supporting our lives. No one who is able to think at all can help going a step farther in thought, and meditating on, if not yet fully comprehending, the Great Source of the original energy of the sun itself.

Section 3.—Conservation of Energy.

280. It appears certain, from modern research, that not a trace of energy has ever been produced or destroyed in the universe (so far as we know it) by human means. Energy, in fact, is as indestructible as matter. A certain amount of energy was associated with the matter of the universe at its creation; and *this precise amount*, and neither more nor less, is present now, although its form may have been changed many times. The energy of sunlight may pass into vital energy, vital energy may pass into heat, heat may be transformed (as in the steam-engine) into mechanical motion, and mechanical motion may be reconverted into heat, as seen in the sparks which appear when the brake is put on to stop a train; but absolutely nothing is lost in the transfer, and nothing is gained.

281. It might seem that energy actually disappears when a cricket-ball is stopped dead by the bat; but it is found that both the ball and the bat become hotter than before. The energy of the ball is, in fact, converted into an exact equivalent of heat-energy, which is soon diffused through the air, but not destroyed. The same change into heat takes place when a bullet is stopped by a target which it does not pierce: the heat evolved is enough to melt the lead, as may often be seen from the shape of the flattened bullet.

282. It might seem, again, that energy was lost when a stone is thrown up to the roof of a house and lodges there; but all the energy which was imparted to the stone when it was thrown up is present in it as statical energy, and remains there until it is dislodged from the roof. When it falls it gives out this energy as kinetic energy in one form or another; for instance, as heat (as in the case of the bullet) when it strikes the ground.

It might seem that energy was created when gunpowder is fired in a gun; but in point of fact the energy was already present in the materials of the gunpowder, put into them in the process of making them, and simply given out when they act on each other.

283. Many attempts have been made to invent a 'perpetual motion' machine—a clock which will go without being wound up; a water-wheel which will pump up its own supply of water; a steam-engine which will do its work without fuel, or some other source of energy. The strongest proof of the doctrine of the conservation of energy is that all such attempts have been utter failures; they are as futile as the attempt of a man standing in a basket to raise himself from the ground by pulling upward at the handles.

284. In fact, all that has been said about the action of forces, in explanation of the Laws of Motion, might be comprehended in the general statement—

> 'Energy cannot be created or destroyed. We can get out of a body the energy which has been put into it, and neither more nor less.'

Section 4.—Measurement of Energy.

285. We cannot *see* Energy, any more than we can see a mind; but we can see and measure the work done in consequence of it. A man's bodily strength and resolution can be fairly gauged by observing how many miles he can walk, or run, or row; how many pounds-weight he can lift from the ground with his hands; or (as in the strength-testing machines often seen at railway stations) how far he can compress a spring by a blow. On a similar principle the amount of available energy in a body is generally measured by observing the amount of mechanical work which is done during its transfer to other bodies.

286. Thus if one cannon-ball will pierce four plates of iron, each 1 inch thick, while another ball will only pierce two such plates, the former ball has twice as much energy as the latter. Again, when a mass of 1 lb. is raised 1 foot from the ground, a certain definite amount of work is done in overcoming the force of gravitation. If a mass of 3 lbs. is lifted 1 foot high, 3 times

as much work is done as in the first case. Also, if 1 lb. is lifted 3 feet high, 3 times as much work is done as in the first case; for it is the same thing as raising 1 lb. through 3 successive stages of 1 foot each.

287. If a cricket-ball is thrown straight up 16 feet by A, 64 feet (or 4 times as far) by B, and 144 feet (or 9 times as far) by C, then B does 4 times as much work with his muscles as A, and C 9 times as much.

288. From these examples it can be seen that the amount of work done in overcoming a resistance varies,

(1) with the mass moved;
(2) with the space through which it is moved;

and that if we multiply the number expressing the mass moved by the number expressing the space through which it is moved, the product will give us a measure of the energy employed in effecting the work.

289. It is convenient to fix upon some definite quantity of work as a unit or standard to compare other quantities with. The unit of work commonly adopted in this country is called a 'foot-pound,' and is

That amount of work which is done in raising a mass of 1 lb. through 1 foot against the attraction of gravitation.

290. As explained above, we have only to multiply the mass of a body expressed in pounds by the height in feet through which it is raised, in order to find the number of foot-pounds of work which have been done, and hence to get a measure of the energy which has been used.

For example—Ten books, each weighing 1 lb., lying on the floor, are raised to a shelf 6 feet above the floor. Here the whole mass moved is 10 lbs. and the height is 6 feet; therefore the work done is (10 × 6 =) 60 foot-pounds. Again, a box weighing 80 lbs. is carried from the ground to a room 20 feet above the ground. Then 80 × 20 = 1600 foot-pounds of work are done by the person who carries it up-stairs.

291. In walking, the whole body is raised through about 4 inches at each step; so that any one who takes 2000 steps in walking a mile, raises his body through (4 × 2000 =) 8000 inches, or 667 feet (nearly) in walking that distance. If he

weighs 140 lbs. (10 stone) he does (140 × 667 =) 93,380 foot-pounds of work.

Relation of Energy to Velocity.

292. We have seen that the amount of work done depends upon the space a body is moved through: we have next to inquire how it depends upon the velocity of movement. Has a locomotive which is moving 2 feet per second twice as much work-power as when it is moving 1 foot per second? The following considerations will show that it has really *much more* than twice the energy.

293. Suppose that the engine is moving 1 foot per second, and that the work it is doing consists in knocking away lumps of snow from the line. Then, if it is made to move 2 feet per second,

(1) It meets twice as many pieces of snow in 1 second, and hence does twice as much work:

(2) It meets each piece with twice the velocity, and therefore knocks it farther away. Here again it does twice the work.

So that altogether it does (2 × 2 =) 4 times the work if it moves with twice the velocity.

Similarly, if it moves with 3 times the velocity, it does (3 × 3 =) 9 times the work, and therefore must have 9 times as much energy as when it was moving 1 foot per second.

Hence we may state it as a law that,

The energy in a body depends upon the square of the velocity with which it is moving.

294. For example—A golf-ball is hit by a club moving at the rate of 8 feet per second, and is driven to a distance of 40 yards. If at another stroke the club hits it with a velocity of 16 feet per second, how far will the ball go? The velocity in the last case is twice as great as before, and therefore the ball will be hit (2^2 =) 4 times the distance; that is, (4 × 40 =) 160 yards.

A hammer falling on a nail with a velocity of 3 feet per second drives it $\frac{1}{8}$ inch into a board. How far will the nail be driven in if the hammer meets it with a velocity of 9 feet per second? In the last case the hammer moves with 3 times the velocity; it therefore has ($3^2 =$) 9 times the energy, and the nail will be driven in ($9 \times \frac{1}{8} =$) $1\frac{1}{8}$ of an inch.

295. This very rapid increase of energy with the speed of a body explains several commonly-observed facts; for example, the great damage done in a collision by an express train compared with that done by a slower train of the same weight. A train moving 60 miles an hour has 9 times the energy of one moving 20 miles an hour, and all this ninefold energy must be got out of it before it stops, either by powerful brakes or by collision with something else.

296. We see also why a cannon-ball has so much greater penetrating power than the gun out of which it comes. The mere *momentum* of the one is, as we have seen (p. 79), exactly equal to that of the other, but the *energy* of the quickly-moving ball is far greater than that of the gun. Suppose that, as in the example given on p. 79, the ball is moving with 120 times the velocity that the gun recoils. Then its energy will, so far as its velocity is concerned, be ($120^2 =$) 14,400 times that of the gun, and hence, although it is much lighter, it has a much greater destructive power. The recoil of a rifle can be borne by the shoulder with no worse effect than an occasional bruise; but the result would be very different if the bullet was driven (by the same charge of powder) against the shoulder, the gun being held with the stock outwards, and allowed to go as far as the recoil would carry it.

Work done by falling Bodies.

297. On the principle of the Conservation of Energy (p. 115), a mass of 1 lb. will, in falling through the distance of 1 foot, do just as much work as was required to raise it 1 foot—that is, it will do 1 foot-pound of work. If it has fallen through 2 feet, it will do 2 foot-pounds of work, and so on.

298. This is well illustrated in the machine used for driving posts or 'piles' into the ground for foundations of bridges, &c. This 'pile-driver' consists of an upright frame in which a heavy iron weight is made to slide up and down (fig. 52). The frame is placed so that the weight rests on the head of the post to be driven in; but the mere weight of the iron is quite insufficient to drive the post into the ground, and all the

strength of several men could not push the post down. The men, however, by pulling at a rope attached to the iron mass and passing over a pulley, raise the weight 8 or 10 feet above the post, and in doing so a certain amount of work is done, and a corresponding amount of energy is transferred from their muscles to the mass, and stored up in it as statical energy. Then the weight is let fall, and all the energy collected in it comes out, with the result of work, when it reaches the head of the post and is stopped; thus the 'pile' is driven some way into the ground, as a nail by a gigantic hammer. Suppose that the block of iron weighs 50 lbs., and that it is raised 10 feet above the head of the pile. Then (50 × 10 =) 500 foot-pounds of work must be done in raising it, and it will do 500 foot-pounds of work in driving down the pile when it falls upon the latter.

Fig. 52.

Relation of Work to Time.

299. The value of work done depends, not only upon *how much* is done, but *how quickly* it is done. A horse is rated more highly as a worker than a donkey or a dog, because it will do the same piece of work much more quickly than either of the latter; though even they would get through the work if we gave them time enough.

300. It is estimated, from experiments, that a first-rate horse can raise 33,000 lbs. (nearly 15 tons) 1 foot high in a minute—that is, can do 33,000 foot-pounds of work *per minute*. This amount of work done in a minute is called one **horse-power**; an expression constantly used in stating the power of engines, &c. When a steam-engine, for instance, is said to be of '8 horse-power,' it is implied that the machine can do, during every minute that it works, (8 × 33,000 =) 264,000 foot-pounds.

ENERGY AND WORK. 121

301. The following table will give an idea of the amount of energy involved in some of the more commonly occurring kinds of work :

Work done per Minute.

	ft.-lbs.
In walking, about.....................................	2,500
" rowing...	3,600
" " at racing speed.............................	6,000
" working a bicycle.....................................	2,300
By an ordinary labourer................................	2,000
" a horse (average).....................................	25,000
" an express engine, when taking a load of 150 tons at the rate of 60 miles an hour	30,000,000

APPENDIX A.

Exact valuation of the energy in a moving body.

302. As already stated (p. 112), when a moving body has its motion stopped or changed, a definite amount of energy comes out of it and goes into the object which stops it; and work is done on the latter.

Thus the energy of a hammer falling on a nail is shown by the extent to which it drives in the nail. This work has been explained in general terms (pp. 117, 118) to vary (a) with the mass, (b) with the square of the velocity of the moving body; and if the work could be done *in an instant*, the energy would be exactly expressed by the product of the mass $\times$ velocity^2. But it takes time to do the work, and during this time the velocity is gradually getting less and less, until there is none left, and then there can be no more work done. Hence, in the first half of the time, more of the work will be done than in the last half of the time. And the whole amount of work which a moving body can do in the time during which its motion is being stopped, will correspond to the *average* or *mean* amount of energy between that which it has at the beginning of the time, and that which it has at the end of the time. Now,

Its energy at the beginning = mass $\times$ velocity^2.
"   "   end   = 0.

And the average or mean of these two quantities is half the sum of them; that is, it

$= \frac{1}{2} \{(\text{mass} \times \text{velocity}^2) + 0 \}$

or $\frac{1}{2} (\text{mass} \times \text{velocity}^2).$

Hence the rule for finding the value of the energy in a moving body may be stated thus—

Multiply the mass by the square of the velocity, and divide the product by 2.

For example: A fives-ball weighing 1¼ oz., and moving 20 feet per second, and a racquet-ball weighing ½ oz., and moving 30 feet per second, strike on a heap of sand; which will go deepest into it?

$$\text{Energy of fives-ball} = (1\tfrac{1}{4} \times 20^2) \div 2 \text{ or } \frac{1\tfrac{1}{4} \times 400}{2} = 250.$$

$$\text{Energy of racquet-ball} = (\tfrac{1}{2} \times 30^2) \div 2 \text{ or } \frac{\tfrac{1}{2} \times 900}{2} = 225.$$

So the fives-ball will penetrate the deepest.

303. Since, on the principle of the conservation of energy (p. 115), just as much energy must go into a body to set it moving, as can be got out of it when its motion is stopped, the above numbers express also the amount of energy employed in throwing the fives-ball and the racquet-ball against the bank.

A cannon-ball weighing 10 lbs. is to have a velocity of 1200 feet per second when it leaves the gun. How much energy is required for this?

$$(10 \times 1200^2) \div 2 = \frac{10 \times 1,440,000}{2} = 7,200,000 \text{ foot-pounds.}$$

Appendix B.

The Pendulum.

304. The simple pendulum is a weight hung from a support by a string or rod (having no appreciable weight itself), so that it can swing easily from side to side. Fig. 53 represents a pendulum of the most common construction. A is the axis or point of suspension; B is the rod; C is the *bob*; consisting of a ball, or a round flattish piece of metal, which is fastened to the rod by a screw behind, by which screw it can be raised or lowered on the rod; DD' is the path or arc which the ball traverses in swinging. When the pendulum is at rest, it hangs perpendicularly, as here represented.

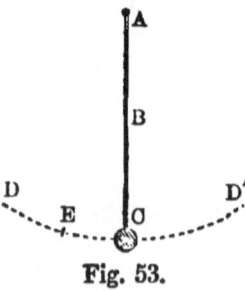

Fig. 53.

305. If the ball is now drawn to one side, as to D, and then let go, gravity urges it downwards, while the

cohesion of the string or rod keeps it at a fixed distance from A. The composition of the two forces makes it describe a descending curve to C, where gravity is completely counteracted by the opposite pull of the rod. But the ball does not stop here; it goes on, by the law of inertia, in the ascending curve CD', until gravity destroys its acquired motion. If friction and the resistance of the air did not interfere, it would take as long to destroy the motion as to generate it, and the ball would reach the same elevation as it started from. But these causes gradually render the ascent less and less, and at last bring the pendulum, when it has no maintaining power, to a state of rest.

306. One sweep of a pendulum from D to D' is called an **oscillation**; and the path it describes, being part of a circle, is called its *arc*. The size or **amplitude** of the oscillation is measured by the number of degrees in the arc, each degree being a 360th part of the whole circle. For reasons which will presently appear, pendulums are generally made to describe small arcs, not exceeding 5° or 6°.

307. The pendulum affords an excellent illustration of statical and kinetic energy. When it is drawn to one side, it is raised a little farther from the centre of the earth, and energy is transferred to it and stored up as statical energy. As it swings back to the perpendicular position, this energy becomes available as kinetic energy, just as in a falling weight (par. 275, p. 113). When it reaches the perpendicular, all the energy imparted to it is in the condition of kinetic energy; but after it has passed this point, the energy available in a kinetic form becomes less and less, being converted by degrees into the statical form. When it pauses at the end of its swing, all the energy is statical once more; and then, on its commencing to move downwards, the change into the kinetic form begins anew.

308. The most remarkable property of the oscillations of the pendulum, and that on which its use as a regulator of movement depends, is that, whether long or short, they are all performed in very nearly the same time. If we observe the vibrations of any body set swinging, we find that though the arc it describes is continually diminishing, there is no sensible shortening of the time in which the single swings are accomplished. As the space to be passed over becomes less, so does the velocity. Galileo, the great astronomer, discovered and investigated this important fact, in 1582 A.D., when only eighteen years old; being led to think on the subject, it is said, by observing the regular swinging of lamps hung from the roof of the cathedral at Pisa.

309. The cause is easily understood. The wider the sweep of the ball, the steeper is its descent at the beginning, and this gives it a greater velocity, and enables it to go over the longer journey in the same time as over a shorter. If we take a moderately short arc, such as CD, fig. 53, the steepness of descent at D is almost exactly double of what it is at E, its middle point; so that a ball beginning its motion at D, moves on an average twice as fast as one starting from E, and thus both arrive at C at the same time.

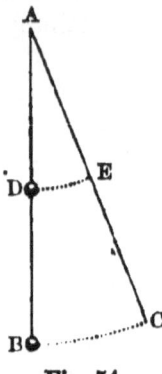

Fig. 54.

310. But it is only short oscillations that are thus isochronous, as it is called; when the arcs are large, the steepness does not increase in exact proportion to the length, and therefore the isochronism is not perfect. Accordingly, pendulums are made to swing in short arcs; and then, though no practical contrivance could make the extent of the oscillations exactly uniform, the times are virtually equal.

311. But though the time of oscillation is independent of the largeness of the arc, it is greatly affected by the length of the pendulum itself. Long pendulums vibrate more slowly than short ones. Though the balls B and D, fig. 54, have the same amplitude of vibration, or go over corresponding arcs, the journey of the one is longer than that of the other. But the steepness of descent, or inclination of the path, is the same in both; therefore B must take longer time to perform its journey than D. We must not, however, conclude that when the length of the pendulum is doubled, the time of oscillation is also doubled. The motion of the pendulum is an accelerated motion; and, as in all other uniformly accelerated motions (see par. 229, p. 92), the spaces described are as the squares of the times. To give double the time of vibration, then, requires the pendulum to be four times as long; treble the time, nine times as long; and so on.

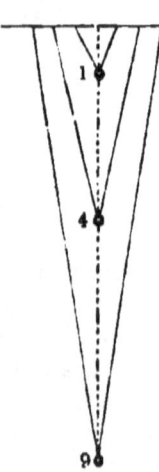

Fig. 55.

312. The truth of this is easily proved by experiment. Suspend three leaden balls on double threads, as in fig. 55, so that the lengths measured in the dotted line may be as 1, 4, and 9. While the lowest ball makes one oscillation, the highest will be found to make three, and the middle ball two.

Length of the Seconds Pendulum.

313. A pendulum of a little more than 39 inches in length (almost exactly one metre), beats once in a second, and one of one-fourth that length beats half-seconds. As a pendulum that beats seconds must always be of the same length, it has been proposed to make it a fixed standard of measure, which can be found again when artificial standards are lost.

314. When we say that the seconds pendulum is always of the same length, we must be understood to speak of the same place. In different places, its length varies. It will be readily conceived that as the motion of the pendulum is caused by gravitation, any alteration in the force of gravitation must alter the rate of its movement. Now the force of gravitation is different in different parts of the earth, being least at the equator, and greatest at the poles, and therefore a pendulum which is to make one swing in a second must be rather shorter at the equator than at the poles. In fact its length must increase as the latitude increases.

Length of a pendulum which makes one swing in a second, at different places:

Spitzbergen............	79° 49′ 58″ N. Lat.,	39·2146 inches.
Edinburgh............	55 58 40 ″	39·1554 ″
London............	51 31 8 ″	39·1390 ″
Jamaica............	17 56 7 ″	39·0350 ″
Sierra Leone............	8 29 28 ″	39·0195 ″

315. How is the length of a pendulum measured? Is it from the point of suspension to the bottom of the ball, or to what point? The answer to this will be plain from what has been said on p. 110 regarding the 'centre of percussion.' We have as yet considered gravitation as acting only on the ball, because the greater part of the matter is concentrated there. But the matter composing the rod is concerned in the movement, and if there were no ball, the rod would form a pendulum of itself. Now, if each particle of matter in the swinging body were at liberty to swing separately, those particles that are nearer to the axis would move more rapidly than those that are farther off. But as the whole cohere in one mass, this tendency is checked; the motion of nearer particles is retarded by the more remote, and the motion of the more remote is accelerated by the nearer. There must, however, be a point dividing the particles that are moving slower than their natural rate

from those that are moving faster than their natural rate—a point which is moving exactly as a particle there situated would move if free to vibrate alone. This point is the **centre of oscillation**. It is evident that the whole of the matter composing a swinging body may be considered as acting at this point; and if it were all concentrated there, the rate of vibration would be the same. The length of a pendulum, then, is measured from the centre of suspension to the centre of oscillation.

316. We may find pretty nearly the centre of oscillation of a common pendulum, or of any swinging body, by suspending in front of it, and from the same axis, a small ball of lead attached to a fine thread. This ball and thread form what is called a **simple pendulum**, because the weight of the thread may be reckoned as nothing, and the matter is as nearly as possible collected in one mass—that is, the ball. Both bodies are now made to swing, and the thread is lengthened or shortened till the two vibrate in exactly the same time; when they come to rest, the centre of the spot on the swinging body covered by the ball is the centre of oscillation.

317. A bar of wood or metal of uniform thickness, may be suspended as a pendulum, and its centre of oscillation determined in the way described. If its position is now reversed, and the centre of oscillation made the centre of suspension, it is found to vibrate in exactly the same time as before. This is expressed by saying that the 'centres of oscillation and suspension are interchangeable.'

318. By making the centre of oscillation the centre of suspension, we shorten the pendulum, and might therefore expect that the time of vibration would be shortened. But in this arrangement a portion of the matter is thrown above the axis, and this acts as a check, and proportionally retards the movement.

319. A pendulum alone, without wheel-work, would form a timekeeper, if we took the trouble to observe and count its vibrations, and if friction and the resistance of the air did not, after a time, bring its motion to an end. The use of the wheel-work in a clock is to answer these two ends—to count and record the swings of the pendulum, and to act as a *maintaining power*—that is, to supply to the pendulum fresh motion in place of what is constantly being destroyed. It is still the pendulum that measures the time.

320. In ordinary clockwork (see fig. 56), the wheels are put in motion by a heavy weight which is attached to a cord wound round

a barrel. One of the wheels is so placed that a piece of metal, fixed on the top of the pendulum, and shaped something like the claw of an anchor, projects its ends, as the pendulum swings, between two teeth of the wheel alternately, first on one side, then on the other. Thus the wheel is held in check, and only one tooth allowed to pass at each swing; and it is evident that an index or seconds hand fixed to the axis of this wheel will record the vibrations of the pendulum. But while the pendulum thus regulates the rate at which the wheel is allowed to move, the teeth of the wheel in contact with the anchor of the pendulum, give it a push as they are disengaged from its ends, and so communicate just as much moving-power to the swinging part as it is losing by friction. Such a contrivance for bringing the pendulum into connection with the wheel-work, is called an *escapement*, of which there are several varieties.

Fig. 56.

321. For adjusting the length of the pendulum, the ball is made to slide on the rod by means of a fine screw. A difference in length of the 1000th part of an inch causes an error of about a second a day. Since all substances are expanded by heat and contracted by cold, changes of temperature must affect the rate of clocks, making them go slower in summer than in winter. **Compensation pendulums**, accordingly, have been contrived, in which expansion in one part is made to counteract expansion in another part.

322. To save space, timepieces are often regulated by pendulums one-fourth the ordinary length, and therefore beating half-seconds. But a long pendulum, with a heavy bob or ball, is desirable where evenness of rate is the object. A pendulum beating two seconds keeps time much more accurately than one beating single seconds.

CHAPTER VII.

MACHINES.

Section 1.—General Principles of Machines.

323. In very many cases it is not convenient or practicable to apply energy directly to do a piece of work. When a load of bricks is to be raised to a scaffolding, we do not force them up by the direct pressure of steam, or by exploding a charge of gunpowder under them. Either a man carries them up a few at a time, or the whole load is raised at once by pulleys and ropes worked by the man, or by an engine. Some apparatus, in fact, is contrived by which the energy necessary to raise the bricks is applied in an indirect but more convenient manner. Such an apparatus is called a 'machine.'

324. **A machine (from μηχάνη, a device) may be defined as a contrivance for transferring energy from one point to another in order to do some particular kind of work conveniently and advantageously.** For example: A clock is a machine in which the force of gravitation pulling a weight downwards is made to turn the hands slowly and uniformly in a circle. A poker is a machine by which a small force directed downward is made to lift a heavy piece of coal upward.

325. In considering the action of machines, the source from which the energy comes is connected with some one part of the apparatus, and is called the **Power**. The work to be done is connected with some other part of the apparatus, and is called the **Resistance**. Thus in a clock the Power is gravitation acting on a weight: the Resistance is the inertia and friction of the wheels and hands. In an engine, the Power is the pressure of the steam applied to the piston; the Resistance is the inertia, friction, &c. of the machinery it drives or the carriages it draws.

Advantage gained in using Machines.

326. It must be borne in mind, to begin with, that a machine cannot really do more work than what corresponds to the energy

which is employed on it. It cannot *create* energy : it can only apply energy in a convenient way for particular purposes.

327. To take a simple case : Suppose that a mass of 3 lbs. has to be raised 1 foot. Then 3 foot-lbs. of work must be done in some way or other; for instance :

(*a*) By raising the whole mass at once with the hands through 1 foot.

(*b*) By dividing it into several parts (say 3 of 1 lb. each), and raising them one by one.

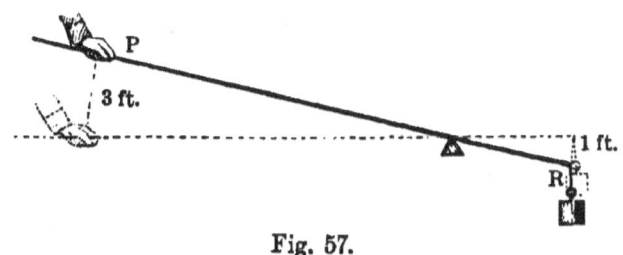

Fig. 57.

(*c*) By using a machine, such as a lever (fig. 57), of such a kind that the point where the Power is applied moves through a greater distance than the point to which the Resistance, that is, the 3 lbs., is attached. Suppose that the point P of the lever moves through 3 times the space that the point R does, when the lever is moved ; then a Power of 1 lb. applied at P will move through 3 feet, and therefore do 3 foot-lbs. of work while R is raised through 1 foot.

328. The advantage of using the method last described is very evident in cases where an extremely large resistance has to be overcome. In fact, a machine, such as a lever or a set of pulleys, will enable a man to lift a block of stone far heavier than he could lift directly with his hands. But yet he will have to move his hands in working the machine through as large a space, and thus do just as much work as if the stone was cut into several pieces, and he lifted them one by one.

329. Most machines are simply contrivances for enabling a small Power or source of energy to move through a great space during its transfer, and thus effect a great deal of work without losing its hold on the Resistance (as it does when the portions of stone are lifted one by one).

Mechanical Advantage.

330. This term means the advantage gained in being able to move a great Resistance by means of a small Power applied in the machine through a large space. In order to estimate it for any given machine, we have only to observe how much space the Power moves through, and compare it with the space through which the Resistance is moved, when the machine is working. The mechanical advantage is represented, in fact, **by the number which expresses how many times the space through which the Power moves is greater than the space through which the Resistance is moved.**

For example: in the lever above mentioned (fig. 57), the hand applied at P moves through 3 feet, while the weight at R is raised 1 foot—that is, the Power moves through 3 times as much space as the Resistance. Hence, the 'mechanical advantage' of this lever is said to be 3; and a man could with it raise a weight three times as great as he could lift with his hands alone.

Rule for finding the mechanical advantage of any machine.—**Divide the space through which the Power moves by the space through which the Resistance is moved; the quotient is the mechanical advantage.**

For example: In using a poker, the end where the hand is applied moves through 1 foot, while the other end placed under the coal moves through 2 inches. Then the mechanical advantage is $\left(\frac{12 \text{ in.}}{2 \text{ in.}} =\right) 6$; and a pressure of 1 lb. will lift a piece of coal 6 lbs. in weight.

331. Sometimes it is more convenient to have the Power move through a small space, while the Resistance is made to move through a large space. Thus, in a clock, the weight only moves a few feet downwards in turning the hands many times round. In such machines there is no mechanical advantage, strictly so called, but the reverse; and the Power must be greater than the Resistance.

332. It is an unfortunate fact that no machine whatever will do all that it ought, by its principle, to do. The power required for working it is always somewhat greater than it should be, as

calculated from the strict mechanical advantage. The reason is, that in all the moving parts of a machine there is some inertia and friction to overcome, and often a great deal; so that more or less additional energy has to be spent in overcoming this, apart from what is used in doing the actual work for which the machine was intended.

333. Machines are usually arranged under four heads, named after the simplest typical machine of each class. They are—

    1. The Pulley.
    2. The Wheel and Axle.
    3. The Lever.
    4. The Inclined Plane.

Section 2.—Pulleys.

334. A **pulley**, fig. 58, is a wheel with a groove in its edge, turning easily in a frame called the 'block.' A cord is placed in the groove, and the Power is attached to one end of this cord.

A pulley is said to be **fixed** when it is attached to a steady support, such as a beam. It is said to be **movable** when it is attached to the Resistance.

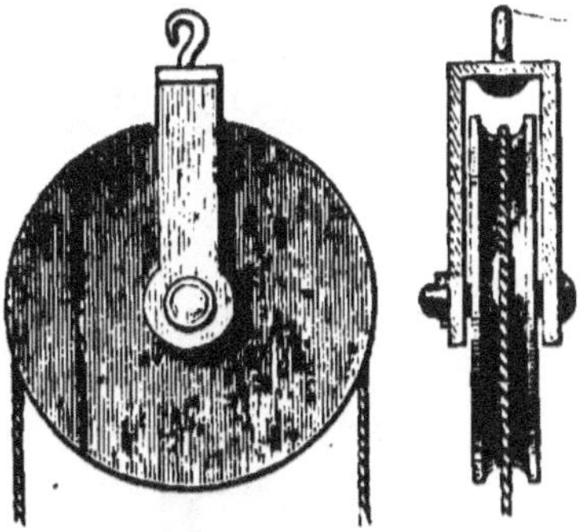

Fig. 58.

Fixed Pulleys.

335. These are used for changing the direction of a force, and give no mechanical advantage, since the Power always moves through the *same* space as the Resistance; as will be plain from fig. 59, in which A is a pulley attached to the beam B. If a weight of 1 lb. (with a small additional weight to overcome friction, &c., as explained in par. 332 above) is attached as the Power to one end, P, of the cord, it will, in falling through 1 foot, raise a Resistance of 1 lb. attached to the other end of the cord, but it will not raise more than 1 lb.; and it will raise this to a height of 1 foot.

336. Such pulleys are to be met with in every house. In
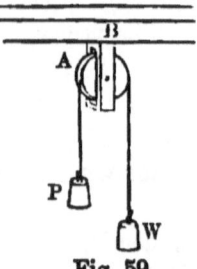
Fig. 59.
sash-windows there is a fixed pulley in the frame at each side; a cord passes round it, one end of which is fixed to the window sash, and the other end to a weight sliding up and down within the frame; so that the sash can be raised and lowered with slight effort. They are also used for drawing curtains, and for opening and shutting windows which are placed too high to be reached with the hand.

Single Movable Pulley.

337. This is a pulley attached to the Resistance, with a cord passing round it, one end of which is tied to a fixed support; the other end is attached to the Power. The simplest arrangement is shown in fig. 60, but the cord is often led over a fixed pulley, as in fig. 61, simply in order to enable the Power to act in a more convenient direction.

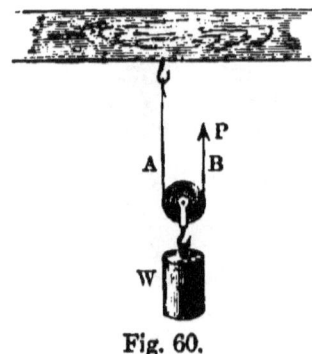
Fig. 60.

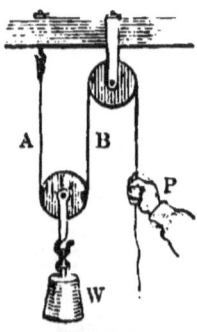
Fig. 61.

338. The mechanical advantage of such a pulley is estimated as follows: The Resistance is obviously held up by two cords, A and B, fig. 60, and in order that it may be raised up 1 inch, *each* of them must be shortened 1 inch. But since they are really parts of the same cord which goes round the pulley, *both* can be thus shortened by simply pulling B through 2 inches; or, what comes to the same thing, by the power at P, fig. 61 (which is part of the same cord), moving through 2

inches. Hence the Power moves through 2 inches, while the Resistance is moved through 1 inch; so there is a mechanical advantage of ($\frac{2}{1} =$) 2. That is, a Power of 1 oz. (with a slight additional weight to overcome friction) will raise a Resistance of 2 oz.

Example.—A log of wood weighing 1 cwt. is to be raised by using a movable pulley; how much power is required?

Since the mechanical advantage is 2, the resistance will be twice the Power; that is, the Power will be half the Resistance; and $\frac{1}{2} \times$ 112 lbs. = 56 lbs.

Therefore a little more than 56 lbs. will do the work.

339. The movable pulley is extensively used in ships for tightening the rigging and moving the yards; it is also often attached to cranes for lifting heavy weights. In clocks the weight is frequently attached to a movable pulley; in this case the weight being the power, there is no mechanical advantage, but the reverse, and a weight twice as heavy as usual is required. But the wheels make twice as many revolutions for a given fall of the weight; so such clocks have the advantage of going for a longer time without being wound up.

Systems of Pulleys.

340. Pulleys are often combined together in various ways, in order to increase the mechanical advantage. Only two of these systems will be described here.

System I.—In this, as shown in fig. 62, (*a*) all the pulleys are movable. (*b*) Each has a separate cord, one end of which is fastened to a fixed support; the other end is tied to the block of the next pulley. (*c*) The cord of the last pulley, C, is attached to the Power; the block of the first pulley, A, is attached to the Resistance.

341. To calculate the mechanical advantage of this system, we must consider that it acts like a number of single movable pulleys, each of which gives (as already explained) a mechanical advantage of 2. Thus,

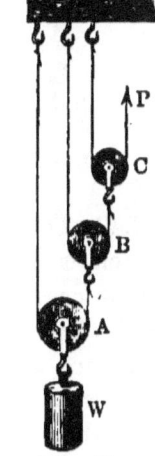

Fig. 62.

The mechanical advantage at A = 2.
" " B = 2 × 2 = 4.
" " C = 4 × 2 = 8.

The Power, then, applied at P, will move a Resistance 8 times as great as itself; but it will only move it through ⅛ of the space.

Rule for finding the mechanical advantage.—Set down 2 as many times as there are movable pulleys, and multiply the numbers together. The product is the mechanical advantage.

Example.—A man capable of exerting a power of 1 cwt. has to raise blocks of stone by the help of 4 movable pulleys; what is the heaviest block he can lift?

$$2 \times 2 \times 2 \times 2 = 16.$$

Hence he can raise a block weighing slightly less than 16 cwt.

342. The disadvantage of this system is, that when it is in action, some of the pulleys soon come up close to one another, and then no more work can be done. Hence it is chiefly used where a great resistance has only to be moved through a small distance; as in tightening the rigging of ships.

System II.—In this, as shown in fig. 63, (*a*) some of the pulleys are in one block, A, which is fixed; the rest are in another block, B, which is attached to the Resistance.

(*b*) There is only one cord, which goes round all the pulleys; one end of it is tied to one of the blocks, the other end is attached to the Power.

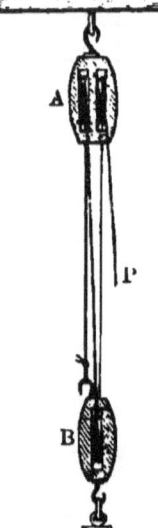

Fig. 63.

343. To calculate the mechanical advantage of this system, which is the most useful and most generally employed of all, we proceed on the same principle as before, of seeing how many cords are employed in holding the resistance, and considering that *each* must be shortened in some way or other, in order that the resistance may be moved.

In the arrangement shown in the figure, there is one pulley in the block to which the resistance is connected, and one end of the cord is also tied to this block. Thus, the resistance is held by 3 cords, and each of these must be shortened 1 inch when the resistance is moved through 1 inch. Now, since the cord going round the pulleys is all in one piece, this shortening of the 3 parts of it can be effected by simply pulling the loose end of it through 3 inches. Hence, if the power is attached to this end, it will move through 3 inches while the resistance is moved through 1 inch. That is, the mechanical advantage is 3. Thus a man capable of lifting 1 cwt. directly, would, by pulling at P, be able to lift a mass of 3 cwt. (nearly).

Rule for finding the mechanical advantage of a set of pulleys arranged on the second system.—**Count the number of cords at the block to which the resistance is attached; this number will express the mechanical advantage.**

Example.—In the set of pulleys shown in fig. 64, it is easy to see that there are 7 cords at the block B. Therefore the mechanical advantage will be 7.

344. This system of pulleys, although it does not give as high a mechanical advantage as the same number of pulley 'sheaves,' or wheels arranged on the first system (as can be easily seen by comparing the examples already given), and although the loss of energy by friction is very great, has yet the important advantage that the resistance can be moved through a considerable distance; in fact, until the two blocks come in contact, or nearly so. It may be seen in use almost wherever heavy masses have to be dealt with, and moved about; in quarries, in housebuilding, in engine and other machinery shops, in dockyards, in ships. In a large vessel, for instance, more than a thousand pulley-blocks are required.

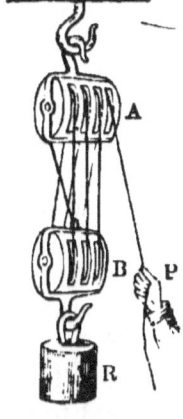

Fig. 64.

Section 3.—The Wheel and Axle.

345. This machine consists of two cylinders of different sizes fixed on the same spindle or axis, so that they turn together. The larger one is called the **wheel** (see fig. 65), and generally has a cord round it, to the end of which the Power is attached.

The smaller one is called the **axle**, and generally has a cord round it, to which the Resistance is attached. The cords are wound in opposite directions, so that when the machine is worked, one cord is wound on, while the other is unwound from, its cylinder.

Fig. 65.

346. The mode in which the relative distances moved through by the Power and the Resistance are estimated, will be understood from the following considerations: Suppose that the machine is turned *once round*, so as to unwind some cord from the wheel. Then the length of cord which is thus removed from the wheel is equal to its circumference; and this expresses the distance moved through by the power. Also, the length of cord which is at the same time wound up on the axle, is equal to its circumference; and this expresses the distance moved through by the resistance. If, for instance, the circumference of the wheel is 12 inches, and the circumference of the axle is 6 inches, then the power moves through $\frac{12}{6}$, or twice as much space as the resistance. Therefore the mechanical advantage of such a wheel and axle would be 2; and a power of 1 lb. applied at P, would raise a resistance of 2 lbs. (nearly) applied at W.

347. We may find the mechanical advantage in an even simpler way than by measuring the circumferences of the wheel and of the axle. For, since the circumference of a circle is always $3\frac{1}{7}$ times its diameter, or $6\frac{2}{7}$ times its radius, it will be sufficient to measure the diameters or the radii of the wheel and axle; and the proportion between these diameters or radii will just as truly represent the proportionate distances passed through by the power and the resistance respectively. Thus, if the diameter of the wheel is 4 times that of the axle, its circumference will be 4 times as great also, and the mechanical advantage of such a machine will be 4.

Rule for finding the mechanical advantage of a wheel and axle.—**Divide the diameter of the wheel by the diameter of the axle; or divide the radius of the wheel by the radius of the axle. The quotient is the mechanical advantage.**

Example.—The diameter of the steering-wheel of a ship's rudder is 3 feet; the diameter of the axle is 4 inches. Here, the diameter of the Wheel of the machine is 36 inches, and that of the Axle is 4 inches; hence $\frac{36}{4} = 9 =$ the mechanical advantage, so that a power of 1 lb. applied at the rim to turn the wheel round will give a strain of 9 lbs. (nearly) on the ropes or chains attached to the tiller.

348. The form of wheel and axle shown in fig. 65 is often very widely departed from in actual practice; so much so, that it is sometimes hard to recognise a machine as really belonging to this class. Perhaps the commonest example of a wheel and axle is a window-blind, in which the blind is raised by unwinding a string from a deep-grooved pulley-wheel fixed at one end of the blind-roller. Here, the roller is an Axle, and the pulley is a Wheel; the resistance is the weight of the blind.

Another common form is the capstan, fig. 66, used on ships for pulling up the anchor, tightening the mooring ropes, &c. In this, the Wheel is

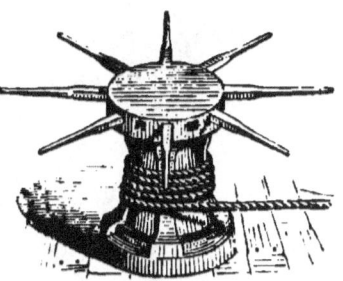

Fig. 66.

not a complete one, all the rim being wanting, while the spokes are there in the shape of wooden bars called 'handspikes,' against the ends of which men push, instead of the power being applied by a cord.

In the ordinary windlass, fig. 67, only one spoke, BC, of the wheel survives, as it were. To the end of this a handle, D, is fitted, to which the power is applied by alternately pushing and pulling it backwards and forwards, up and down. Such a machine is used in raising buckets of water from deep wells; in raising coal and ore from mines; and, in conjunc-

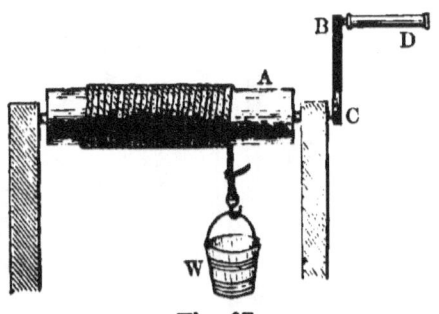

Fig. 67.

tion with pulleys, for lifting materials to the top of scaffolding.

138 ELEMENTARY DYNAMICS.

In the bicycle, fig. 68, the power is applied to a treadle, which corresponds to the axle or smaller cylinder of fig. 65. Thus, there is no mechanical advantage; the power of the muscles is, in fact, applied at a disadvantage, and hence there is much difficulty in working such a machine along anything but a hard level road. But it has the practical convenience that, by moving the foot through a small distance, the edge of the large wheel is made to travel over a much greater distance of road. The crank of an engine, fig. 69, or a lathe, or a sewing-machine, acts on the same principle. Other common examples of the application of the wheel and axle are: A waterwheel (fig. 70), a paddle-wheel of a steamer, a treadmill, a door handle; the 'rack and pinion' used in raising the sluices of locks, or raising the wick of a lamp, or working an air-pump,

Fig. 68.

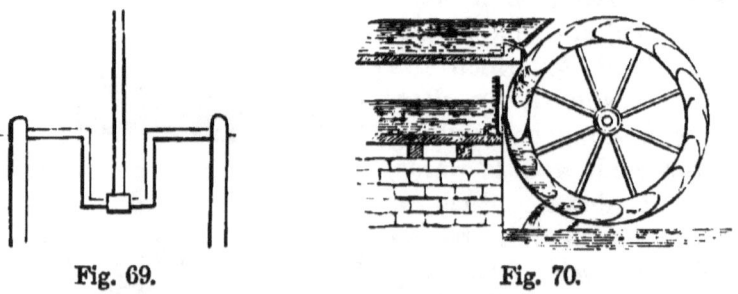

Fig. 69.   Fig. 70.

fig. 71. In this form, the circumference of the axle is cut into teeth or 'cogs'; it is then called a **pinion**, and these cogs catch

MACHINES. 139

against similar cogs cut in a straight rod called the **rack**, which takes the place of the more usual cord attached to the resistance.

349. To obtain greater mechanical advantage, several wheels and axles are sometimes connected together by cutting cogs in

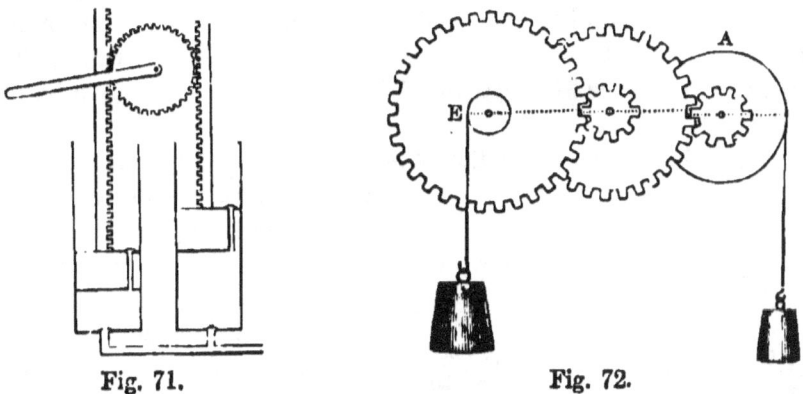

Fig. 71.   Fig. 72.

the circumference of the first axle, so as to work or 'gear' into cogs cut in the circumference of the next wheel. The axle of this latter may be made similarly to gear into another wheel,

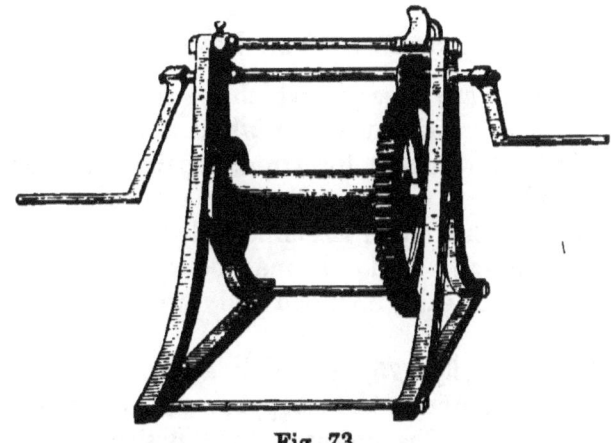

Fig. 73.

and so on, as shown in fig. 72. Such an arrangement is called a 'train of wheels,' and is used for two distinct purposes.

(1) To gain *power*: for which purpose the power is applied to the wheel, A, of the first axle, and the resistance is connected

with the axle, E, of the last wheel. The powerful windlass called a **crab**, fig. 73, is an example of this.

(2) To gain *speed*. In this case, as shown in fig. 72, the power is applied to the axle, E, of the last wheel, and the resistance is connected with the wheel, A, of the first axle. The wheelwork of clocks and watches affords an excellent illustration of this principle. In an ordinary watch, the barrel containing the spring only makes $3\tfrac{1}{2}$ turns in 24 hours, while the seconds hand makes 1440 turns.

350. Wheels and axles may also be connected by an endless cord or strap, passing round both, and tightened until there is sufficient friction to prevent its slipping. Lathes and sewing-machines are worked in this way, and the various machines in a mill are driven by straps passing round pulleys or 'drums,' on a long shaft worked by the engine, fig. 74.

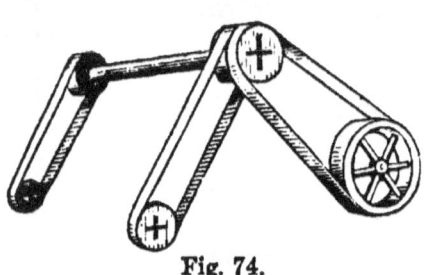

Fig. 74.

Section 4.—The Lever.

351. There are many cases in which we only want to move a body through a short distance; as when a large paving-stone has to be lifted a few inches for street repairs. It would be a cumbrous expedient to set up pulleys or a windlass for such a purpose, and a much simpler machine called a **lever** (Lat. *levare*, 'to raise') is generally used. It may be looked upon as essentially a wheel and axle intended only to turn a little way round.

352. A **lever** (see figs. 75, 76, 77) is a strong, stiff rod, movable at one point round a firm support, called a **fulcrum** (Lat. *fulcire*, to support). The Power and the Resistance are applied at two different points on this rod.

353. There are three different orders of levers, the distinction between them depending on whether the fulcrum, the Resistance, or the Power, is put between the two ends of the rod. Thus we have—

MACHINES. 141

In the First Order, fig. 75 :

Power at one end ;
Resistance at the other end ;
Fulcrum between them.

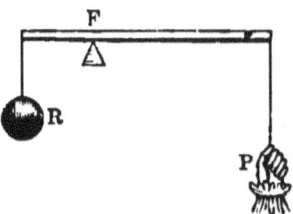

Fig. 75.

In the Second Order, fig. 76 :

Power at one end ;
Fulcrum at the other end ;
Resistance between them.

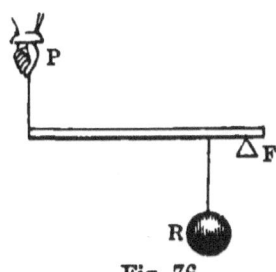

Fig. 76.

In the Third Order, fig. 77 :

Resistance at one end ;
Fulcrum at the other end ;
Power between them.

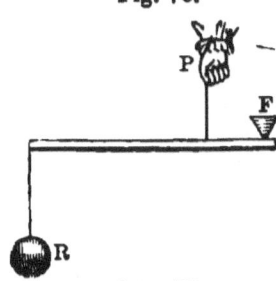

Fig. 77.

354. The lever is considered as made up of two parts which are called the **arms**: the length of these being in all cases measured from the fulcrum. Thus,

The distance from the Power   to the fulcrum is one arm.
 "   "   "   Resistance   "   "   the other arm.

[In the following examples, the lever will be assumed in all cases to have its arms equally balanced before any work is done ; so that the weight of the rod itself may be neglected.]

355. The mechanical advantage of the lever is calculated on the same principle as that of the wheel and axle ; one arm of the lever being considered as the radius of the wheel, and the other arm as the radius of the axle. Thus, if the Power-arm is twice

J

as long as the Resistance-arm, as in fig. 78, the Power will move through twice as much space as the Resistance, when the lever is being used; and there will be a mechanical advantage of 2.

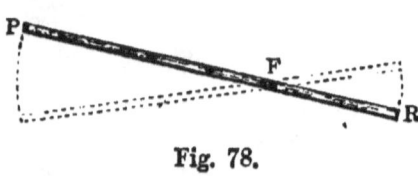

Fig. 78.

Rule for finding the mechanical advantage of any lever.—**Divide the length of the Power-arm by the length of the Resistance-arm; the quotient is the mechanical advantage of the lever.**

Example.—In a lever of the first order, the power-arm is 30 inches long, the resistance-arm is 6 inches long; what work could be done with a power of 2 lbs.? Dividing 30 by 6, we have a quotient of 5 as the mechanical advantage: so that a resistance of (5 × 2 lbs. =) 10 lbs. could be moved.

356. It must be observed that the ends of the arms of the lever move in the circumferences of circles of which the fulcrum is the centre, as indicated in fig. 79; and that, when the resistance is simply a weight to be lifted straight up, most of the work is done along a perpendicular line, AB, passing through its centre of gravity. In such cases it is easily seen that the real acting arm of the lever is not FR, but the length of the shortest line that can be drawn from the fulcrum to the perpendicular AB—that is, the line FR' at right angles to AB. This line is generally shorter than FR, and so the mechanical advantage is greater in this position of the lever. As the lever comes up to the horizontal position, the length of the acting arm FR' increases until it becomes equal to FR: if the lever is moved farther up, FR' diminishes again. The same is true, of course, of the other arm, when the power can only act in one direction; but when the power is applied by the hand, it is continually changing its line of action,

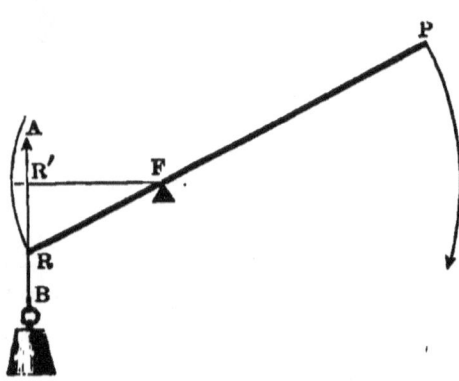

Fig. 79.

as when a windlass handle is worked, and then the acting length of the power-arm remains the same.

Moment of a Force.

357. When a force is used to turn a body round some point as a centre, the length of such a line as FR' in fig. 79—that is, of the *shortest* line which can be drawn from the centre of rotation to the line of action of the force—expresses what is called the **moment** of the force; that is, its effect in turning the body round the given centre.

Levers of the First Order.

358. There are many common examples of levers of the first order. For instance, a poker; the Power being the muscular energy of the arm and hand, the fulcrum being the bar of the grate, while the Resistance is the piece of coal to be lifted; a crowbar, when used as shown in fig. 80, to lift heavy weights; a spade, when used to detach a portion of earth from the main mass by forcing back the handle; a pair of scissors, or pincers, in which we

Fig. 80.

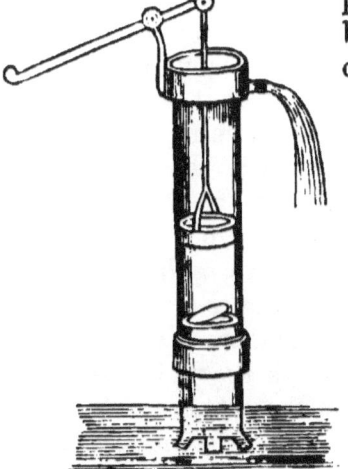

Fig. 81.

Fig. 82.

have a double lever, the common fulcrum being the joint on which the blades turn; a pump handle, fig. 81.

359. In the common balance, or 'pair of scales,' fig. 82, we

have a lever with arms of equal length, so that there is no mechanical advantage. This lever is called the **beam**, and from its ends, at precisely equal distances from the middle point or fulcrum, are hung pans or **scales**. It is used in 'weighing' a thing—that is, in finding out how much the earth attracts it, by balancing it against some standard weight, such as a pound. For when the thing to be weighed is put into one scale, there can only be equilibrium—that is, the beam can only remain horizontal—when there is an *equal* weight in the other scale, because the arms of the lever from which the scales are hung are made exactly equal in length.

360. In the 'steelyard,' fig. 83, we have a lever in which one of the arms can be made to vary in length. Only one weight is used, which is made to slide along the beam; and a substance is weighed by putting it into the scale W, and seeing where the weight P has to be placed on the beam in order to balance it. Suppose that the weight P is 1 lb.; then if it is put just as far from C, the fulcrum, as A is from C on the other side, the arms of the lever are of equal length, and if the substance put into the scale produces equilibrium, it must weigh 1 lb. If the substance just balances P when the latter is placed on the beam twice as far from C as C is from A, it must weigh 2 lbs., for the power-arm PC is now twice as long as the resistance-arm CA, and there is a mechanical advantage of 2. The beam is graduated as shown in the figure, and stamped with numbers which show the actual weight of the substance in the scale-pan corresponding to different positions of P. Letter-weighing machines are often made on the same principle.

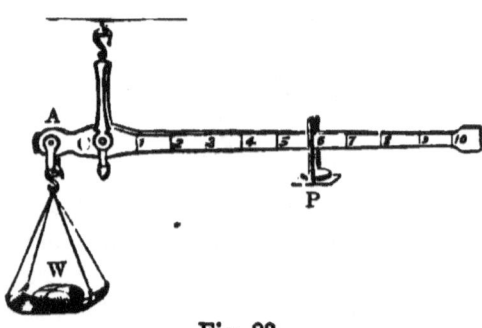

Fig. 83.

Levers of the Second Order.

361. In these, as is obvious from fig. 84, there must always be a mechanical advantage, because the Power is always farther

from the fulcrum than the Resistance is. The amount of mechanical advantage is calculated in the same way as for levers of the first order; it being borne in mind that the power-arm is the distance from P to F, and the resistance-arm is the distance from R to F.

For example, in one of such levers, the distance from the power to the fulcrum is 30 inches, and the distance from the resistance to the fulcrum is 6 inches. Then,

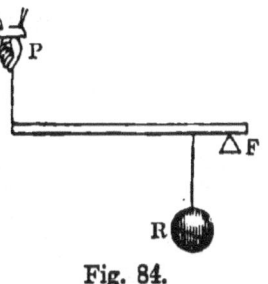

Fig. 84.

$$\frac{\text{Length of power-arm}}{\text{Length of resistance-arm}} = \tfrac{30}{6} = 5.$$

So the mechanical advantage is 5; and a man who exerted a force which would lift 1 cwt. directly, could by this lever raise a weight of 5 cwt. (nearly).

362. As examples of levers of the second order, the following

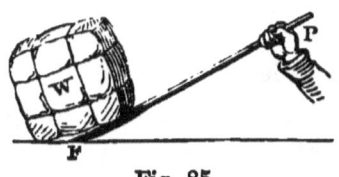

Fig. 85.

may be taken: A crowbar, when used as shown in fig. 85. An oar; in which the fulcrum is the water against which the blade of the oar presses, the power is applied by the hand at the inner end of the oar, and the resistance is the inertia and friction of the boat (and in some cases, of course, the force of the stream) applied at the rowlock. A wheel-barrow, fig. 86; in which the fulcrum is the axis of the wheel, the power is applied near the end of the handle, and the resistance is the weight of the barrow and the load in it. A door or gate; in which the fulcrum is the hinges, the power is applied in opening or shutting the door, and the resistance is the inertia and friction of the door (gravitation, except in the case of a trap-door, not being directly concerned). A pair

Fig. 86.

Fig. 87.

of nutcrackers, fig. 87, which, as is easily seen, are a double lever; the fulcrum being the joint which connects the arms, the power is applied by the hand pressing the arms together, and the resistance is the cohesion of the nut.

363. The action of this kind of lever is also shown when a load is being carried on a pole by two men, each bearing one end of the pole, fig. 88. Each man acts as the power in lifting the weight, and at the same time the shoulder of each serves as a fulcrum for the lever worked by the other. If the weight hangs fairly from the middle of the pole, each man will bear just half the burden; but if the weight is slipped along towards one end, then the man to whom it is nearest supports a greater load than the other.

Fig. 88.

Levers of the Third Order.

364. In these, as shown in fig. 89, there obviously can never be any mechanical advantage at all, since the resistance, being at the end, is always farther from the fulcrum than the power, and therefore it must move through a greater space than the power. Hence the power must always necessarily be greater than the resistance, and this kind of lever is chiefly used where there is plenty of energy available, and it is required to move anything through a large space.

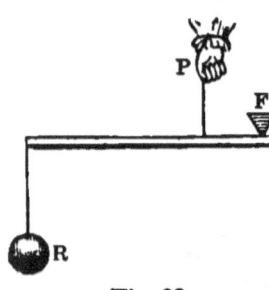

Fig. 89.

The 'mechanical disadvantage,' as it may be called, is found in the usual way; the power-arm being the distance from P to F, and the resistance-arm the distance from R to F. Suppose, for instance, that the length from P to F is 4 inches, and from R to F 20 inches, then,

$$\frac{\text{Power-arm}}{\text{Resistance-arm}} = \tfrac{4}{20} = \tfrac{1}{5}.$$

So that the resistance can only be 1/5 the power, or the power must be 5 times the resistance. But this resistance will be moved through 5 times as much space as the power passes through.

365. Nearly every joint in the human body affords an illustration of this kind of lever. Thus the principle of the action of the elbow-joint, when the arm is bent, is shown in fig. 90. The fulcrum is the elbow-joint itself, at F; the power is supplied by the forcible contraction of a strong muscle (the *biceps*), one end of which is attached by tendons to a bone of the forearm, B, near the joint, while its other end is attached to the shoulder at S (in the figure a weight is shown, passing over a pulley at S,

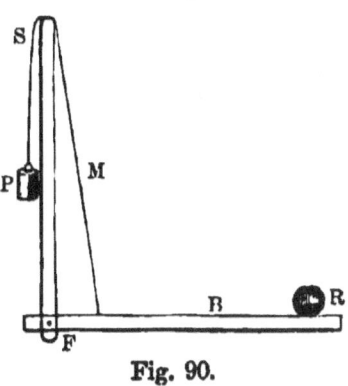

Fig. 90.

merely to illustrate the mode of action); the resistance is anything to be moved by the hand. The actual arrangement of bones and muscles of the arm is shown in fig. 91. The work of straightening out the arm when bent is done by a

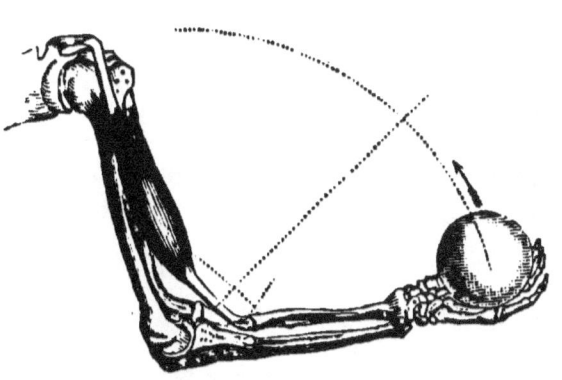

Fig. 91.

muscle lying behind the elbow-joint, and passing over it, as over an axle: so the extension of the arm is effected by a machine on the principle of the wheel and axle.

Since nearly all the muscles are attached very near the joints of the limbs they move, the power-arms of these human levers are very short as compared with the resistance arms: and hence the energy actually concerned in doing such work as the strength of a man enables him to do, must be enormous. Take, for instance, the work implied in lifting 1 cwt. from the ground by bending the arm at the elbow. The distance from the middle of the hand to the elbow-joint may be taken as about 15 inches: the biceps muscle is attached about 1 inch from the joint. Hence the mechanical disadvantage is $\frac{1}{15}$—that is, the muscle in contracting must exert a force which would raise 15 cwt. if applied directly.

On the other hand, since the space moved through by the resistance is comparatively very great, we gain from this arrangement of the limbs and muscles the real and important advantage of being able by a small movement of the muscles to move the limbs far and quickly; as in hitting, throwing, running, playing the piano, &c.

366. A cricket-bat is another example of a lever of the third order; acting, in fact, in some cases like a mere prolongation of the arm; though more often, as in blocking a ball, the left hand is held steady as the fulcrum, and the power is applied chiefly by the right hand pressing on the bat farther down the handle. In the use of a spade for throwing up soil, and of a pitchfork for lifting hay, a similar action is observable, one hand serving as the fulcrum while the power is applied mainly by the other. In practice, however, both hands move a little in all the above cases, so we have an action of levers of both the first and the third order. In using a pencil or pen, and a pair of sugar-tongs or ordinary tongs, force is applied to levers of a similar kind.

SECTION 5.—THE INCLINED PLANE.

367. This may be described as a smooth, flat surface, placed obliquely to the direction in which the resistance has to be moved. Thus, to take the commonest case, that of a weight such as W, fig. 92, to be lifted vertically upwards, l represents an inclined plane making some angle less than a right angle with a vertical direction.

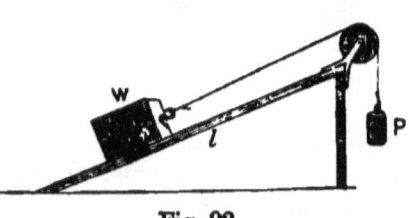

Fig. 92.

Suppose that the resistance is a weight of 1 lb., and that it has to be raised to a level 1 foot above the place where it is. Then 1 foot-lb. of work is required; and this may be done either (*a*) by a power sufficient to lift it straight up; or (*b*) by a smaller power moving it up a long slope to the required level. If the slope is 2 feet long, then the power moves through 2 feet instead of 1 foot in raising the weight; so that a mechanical advantage of 2 is gained.

368. It is clear that the longer the plane is, compared with the distance through which the resistance is moved in the required direction, the greater will be the mechanical advantage gained; and the way of calculating its exact value will be seen from what follows.

Let A, fig. 93, be the end of the plane where the resistance is placed. Through the other end, B, draw a line, CB, in the direction in which the resistance is to be moved; and from A draw AC perpendicular to BC. Then BC is the distance through which the resistance is actually moved in the required direction by the power. It is generally called the 'height' of the inclined plane (although, of course, the machine will act in any direction, and not merely in lifting bodies).

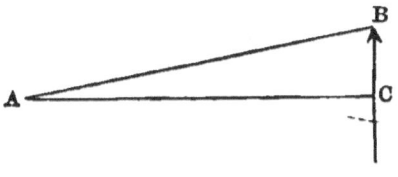

Fig. 93.

Now, when the power acts along the plane as in fig. 92, the length of the plane is the distance through which it moves, and the 'height' of the plane is the distance through which the resistance is moved in the required direction. Hence we get the following rule:

Rule for finding the mechanical advantage of an inclined plane, when the power acts in the direction of the length of the plane.—**Divide the length of the plane by its height; the quotient is the mechanical advantage.**

Example.—An inclined plane is 18 inches long, and 6 inches high; what will be the mechanical advantage?

$$\frac{\text{Length of plane}}{\text{Height of plane}} = \frac{18}{6} = 3.$$

Hence the mechanical advantage will be 3.

369. The commonest example of an inclined plane is a road leading up a hill. A carriage drawn along it is raised more and more from the centre of the earth, and hence a greater power must be used than is necessary to draw it along a level road. Sometimes the road is made to wind as in fig. 94, instead of going straight up the hill, in order to make the inclined plane longer, and thus increase the mechanical advantage: so that a single horse may be able to draw a heavily-loaded waggon up it.

Fig. 94.

The slope of the road is generally expressed by saying how much it rises in a certain length. For example—an incline of '1 in 100' means that if the plane were 100 feet long, the top would be 1 foot above the level of the lower end; and in this case the mechanical advantage would be 100, whatever the actual length of the plane might be. Inclines on a railway seldom exceed a 'gradient' of 1 in 60; but on ordinary roads the gradient is sometimes as steep as 1 in 7 or 8.

370. In order to raise a heavy cask into a cart, an inclined plane is often extemporised by laying planks sloping upwards from the ground to the bottom of the cart, up which the cask is rolled. The immense stones of which the Pyramids are built, were probably raised up to their places by a contrivance of this kind.

371. Sometimes the power is applied, not along the plane, but in a direction at right angles to that in which the resistance is to be moved—that is, in the direction of the line AC, fig. 93, which is often referred to as the 'base' of the plane. Then, of

course, the power moves through the distance AC in moving the resistance through the distance CB, and,

$$\frac{\text{Base of the plane}}{\text{Height of the plane}} = \text{the mechanical advantage.}$$

A good example of this is afforded by the 'wedge,' fig. 95, which really consists of two inclined planes put base to base. The resistance is put at the thinnest part of the wedge, A, and the power is applied in the direction of the base CA. It moves the resistance by shifting the plane along it; so the wedge is simply a movable inclined plane.

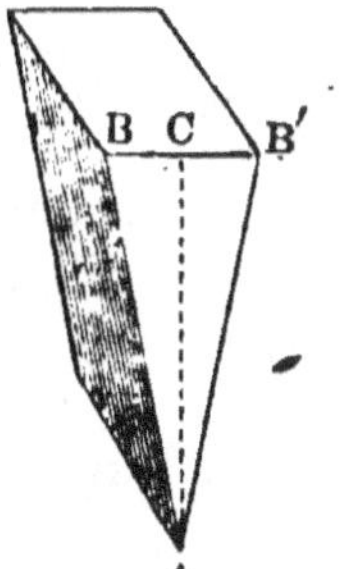

372. To find the mechanical advantage of a wedge, we must observe that the resistance is moved through the space BB', while the power moves through the space CA. Hence—

Rule for finding the mechanical advantage of a wedge.—**Divide the length of the wedge, measured along its middle line, by its thickness at the blunt end; the quotient is the mechanical advantage.**

Fig. 95.

Example.—If the length of a wedge is 6 inches, and its greatest thickness is 1 inch, then $\frac{6}{1} = 6$. So the mechanical advantage is 6.

Usually the wedge is made very long in proportion to its thickness, so the mechanical advantage gained is theoretically very great; but a large amount of energy is spent in overcoming the friction between the wedge and the material into which it is being driven,* so that practically not more than half the proper mechanical advantage is gained.

373. A common use of the wedge is for splitting timber, as illustrated in fig. 96; also for detaching blocks of stone in quarries, a series of wedges being driven in along the line in which the stone is to be split off from the main mass. Ships are raised in docks by driving in wedges under them.

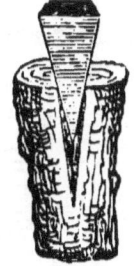

Fig. 96.

374. But there are still commoner instances of its

---

* This friction, however, serves a useful purpose, since the wedge thus holds its place in the material, so that it can be driven farther and farther in.

employment, for a little observation will show that all cutting and boring instruments, ploughs, axes, chisels, saws, knives, scissors, &c., act on the principle of this simple 'machine'; the finest surgeon's lancet no less than the roughest pickaxe. Indeed, the wedge not only cuts our materials into shape, but also holds them together when shaped; for nails and pins are only square or round wedges, driven in and holding their places by friction.

375. Another modification of the inclined plane is the screw, fig. 97, which consists of a cylinder with a raised ridge, called the 'thread,' running round it in a spiral line. It works in a hollow cylinder called the nut, with spiral grooves cut in it which fit the threads of the screw. When *either* the nut *or* the screw is turned (the other being fixed), the nut travels slowly from end to end of the screw.

376. The screw is really an inclined plane wound round a cylinder (somewhat like the road in fig. 94), as indicated in fig. 98. If the distance between one thread and the next

Fig. 98.

(which is called the 'pitch' of the screw) is small, the slope of the plane is very gradual, and a great mechanical advantage is gained. To calculate this, we must notice that the 'base'

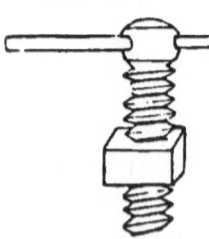

Fig. 99.

of the inclined plane is the end of the cylinder on which the screw is formed, or any surface at right angles to the length of the cylinder. Thus the power which turns the screw or the nut is applied parallel to the base of the plane. Now suppose that the nut is attached to the resistance, and prevented from turning while the power is applied to the screw. When the screw has been turned once round, the nut (and with it the resistance) has been moved through a distance equal to that between one thread and the next (called the 'pitch' of the screw), while the power (if it acts at the edge of the cylinder) has moved through a space equal to the circumference of the cylinder. But the power is, in practice, applied, not to any point on the cylinder, whether in the nut or screw, but to the edge of a wheel, or the end of a handle fixed to the screw or nut, as in fig. 99; and so the circumference of this wheel, or of the circle in which the end of the handle moves, must be taken into account in calculating the mechanical advantage.

Rule for finding the mechanical advantage of the screw.—**Divide the length of the circumference of the circle in which the power moves by the distance between one thread of the screw and the next thread; the quotient is the mechanical advantage.**

Example.—In a screw-press, such as that shown in fig. 100 below, the length of the handle is 21 inches, and the distance between two threads of the screw—that is, the 'pitch' of the screw—is 1 inch: find the mechanical advantage.

Here the radius of the circle in which the power moves is 21 inches; therefore the circumference of the circle will be $6\frac{2}{7}$ times this, or ($6\frac{2}{7} \times 21 =$) 132 inches. Then,

$$\frac{\text{Circumference of circle}}{\text{Pitch of screw}} = \frac{132}{1} = 132.$$

So the mechanical advantage is **132.**

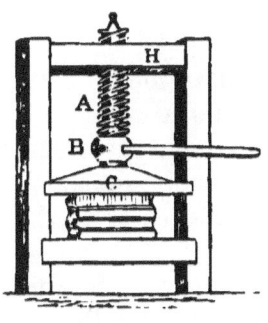

Fig. 100.

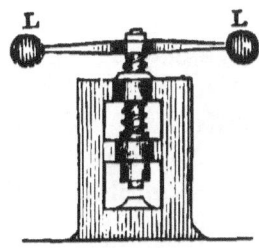

Fig. 101.

By making the pitch of the screw very fine, and applying the power at the end of a long lever, an enormous mechanical advantage can be obtained; at the same time, however, nearly one-half of this is lost by friction.

377. One useful application of the screw is seen in the 'screw-press,' fig. 100, in which the nut, H, is fixed in a strong frame, and the screw, A, is turned round by a lever placed in holes shown at B. As the screw descends, its lower end presses upon a thick plate, C, below which are placed the books or packets of paper which are to be compressed. A similar kind of press is used in cheese-making and cider-making. Coins are stamped by the more powerful press shown in fig. 101, in which heavy weights, L, L, are attached to the end of the levers which work the screw. These levers are whirled quickly round, and the energy thus accumulated in the mass is expended in one powerful blow upon the dies between which the blank disc of metal is compressed.

378. Simpler illustrations of the screw are found in the 'bolts and nuts,' fig. 102, used for clamping together the beams of a roof and the various parts of a machine. About 800 of these are used in the construction of a single locomotive engine. In the common 'wood-screw,' fig. 103, the threads are thin and sharp, so that they cut into the wood like a knife, and make grooves for themselves as the screw is turned round by the screw-driver.

Fig. 102. Fig. 103.

Section 6.

379. We may, in conclusion, turn our attention for a moment to one of the finest of modern machines, the locomotive engine (see frontispiece), and see how it illustrates in its construction and work the properties of matter, the laws of motion, and the principles of machines, which have been treated of in the foregoing pages.

380. The three states of matter are illustrated in the solid framework (the skeleton, as it were) of the engine, the water in the boiler, and the steam into which it is converted by the heat of the fire.

381. The various kinds of cohesion of matter are shown in

the strong steel piston rods, the tough iron framework, the elastic springs, the perfectly elastic steam.

382. The weight of modern engines is enormous. While Stephenson's original engine, the 'Rocket,' only weighed four tons and a quarter, an express engine, as now made, weighs forty or even fifty tons. A single look will show how even the strongest steel rails, on the most solidly constructed road, bend under its weight.

383. Owing to this great mass, the momentum of an engine, especially when travelling at a high velocity, is very great indeed. Engines have been known to start off of their own accord, through some negligence, and go right through the brick wall of the engine-shed with perfect ease, although the speed attained could not have been high.

384. Yet an engine cannot of itself move a single inch. Energy must be supplied in some form; and this is done by the burning of the fuel—that is, its combination with the oxygen of the air. Energy is thus made available in the form of heat, which is transferred to the water, turning it into steam, putting its molecules, in fact, into such rapid motion that they press strongly against the sides of the boiler and against the pistons of the engine. These latter are driven to and fro, and through the medium of the piston rods and connecting rods turn the cranks round, and with them the driving-wheels with which they are connected. Thus the straight to-and-fro motion caused by the steam is converted first into rotatory motion of the wheels, and then into continuous motion in one direction of the engine and its load along the line.

385. The force thus continuously acting causes a velocity which would, if it were not for opposing forces, increase continuously (uniformly accelerated motion); and when once the inertia of the mass is overcome, the whole would go on moving, according to the first Law of Motion, even though the steam was shut off. But owing to resistance of the air and friction of the numerous moving parts, the velocity is not accelerated beyond a certain point, where the various forces are in equilibrium. It then becomes uniform; and if the steam is shut off, it is retarded and ultimately ceases. If more friction is brought into action by means of the brake, the energy of the moving

mass passes still more quickly into the form of heat, as the sparks flying from the brake-blocks abundantly testify.

386. The laws of Centrifugal Tendency are illustrated by the pressure against the outside rail when the engine goes round a curve; a pressure which, at high velocities, may become so great as to displace the rail or cause the wheel to override it. Hence this rail is raised so as to tilt the engine and throw the centre of gravity so far inwards that one of the components into which the force of gravitation may be then resolved, pulls the whole mass inwards sufficiently to counteract the centrifugal tendency.

387. The Composition of Forces is also illustrated in cases where the engine is going up or down an incline. Here gravitation, which primarily is a single force pulling the mass straight downwards, is resolved into two components, one of which acts along the plane and either accelerates or retards the motion of the train.

388. The third Law of Motion is illustrated by the action of the steam in the cylinder. It presses just as strongly against the ends of the cylinder as against the piston, and only moves the latter because it is most easily moved. When the engine runs up against an obstacle, such as a mass of earth or brick, or another train, it suffers damage itself as well as the obstacle, and the comparative masses and momenta of the two decide which suffers most. If the obstacle is relatively light, such as a block of stone, or a gate, or a cow, it is usually cleared out of the way by the massive engine.

389. In order that the engine may run steadily and safely, it is essential that the wheel-base should be broad and the centre of gravity as low as possible. Hence the boiler is made in the form of a long horizontal cylinder, not placed over the furnace as usual, but nearly on the same level with it; the water being heated by a multitude of tubes within the boiler through which the flame passes. The machinery is all packed below the boiler, as near the rails as safety will allow. Thus the equilibrium is extremely stable, and the engine will run through a hurricane without being blown over.

390. Every kind of Mechanical Power, except perhaps the Pulley, is fully employed in the engine. The Wheel and Axle

appear in the cranks and wheels (the crank being technically the Axle, and the driving-wheel the Wheel of the machine); also in the handles of the numerous stopcocks employed. The Lever appears in the starting lever, the reversing lever, the 'link motion' which works the slide valves for admitting steam to the cylinders, and the long arm by which the safety valve is held down. The Inclined Plane is seen in the wedges or 'cotters' which tighten up the bearings; and in the multitude of screws employed throughout the machine.

391. As an illustration of the principles of Energy and Work, the locomotive has been already often referred to. It has been shown that the energy stored up in a statical form in the coal and the oxygen of the air becomes kinetic when they combine; at first appearing in the form of heat, then as swift mechanical motion of the whole mass. While the engine is running, energy is constantly being transferred to the molecules of the air, of the rails, and of the machinery; appearing, in fact, eventually as heat, which unfortunately is lost to us as far as useful work is concerned.

392. It is disappointing to reflect how very imperfect a machine even the best steam-engine is. Out of the whole energy set free by the combustion of the coal, not more than *one-sixteenth* is, in the most scientifically constructed engine, convertible into useful mechanical work. All the rest is dissipated and lost (to us) in the form of heat.

393. It is, in fact, easy to convert energy of mechanical motion entirely into the form of heat; but it is impossible, with our present means, to convert heat-energy entirely into mechanical motion. Thus, during all movements, whether of the human body or of inanimate machines, some energy is continually passing into a less available form, namely, heat; and the investigations of science teach us that, if the present course of things continues, we must look forward to a time when so much of the energy present on the earth will have been degraded, as it were, into the form of heat, that all things will be at the same extremely high temperature, and life and work will be impossible.

APPENDIX.

THE METRIC SYSTEM OF MEASURES AND WEIGHTS.

Measure means the space over which anything extends.

Weight means the pressure of bodies towards the centre of the earth caused by the force of gravitation.

The sizes and weights of things are usually expressed in terms of some 'unit' or standard amount of space or pressure, such as a 'foot,' a 'yard,' a 'metre,' a 'pound,' or a 'gramme.' Thus, in saying that a rod is six feet long, we mean that it extends in length over six times the space of the unit of length which we call a 'foot.' Again, in saying that a piece of lead weighs two pounds, we mean that it presses towards the earth's centre with twice as much force as a particular piece of matter which we call a 'pound-weight.'

In selecting a unit for practical purposes, we are mainly guided by three considerations:

1. The unit must be of such a kind that another exactly similar one could be easily obtained, if the original unit was lost or damaged.

2. It must not be very large or very small; otherwise in common use we should constantly have to deal with awkward fractions or inconveniently large multiples of it.

3. It must have other measures and weights derived from it by the simplest possible methods of multiplication and division.

APPENDIX.

The unit, or starting point, of the metric system (which is now almost universally employed in scientific work) is the METRE, which is a length of one forty-millionth part of the circumference of the earth, measured under the meridian of Paris.

The actual metre is a flat bar of platinum, about 39.4 inches long, each end of which is exactly at right angles to the length of the bar; the distance between the ends at the temperature of freezing water is defined to be one metre. Several extremely accurate copies of this have been made, and it is probable that scientific men will be content with these copies, and other copies of them, without again deriving the unit from an actual measurement of the earth.

MEASURES OF LENGTH.

In deriving other measures of length from the metre, only the number 10 and its multiples are employed; and names are selected which denote the relation of the particular measure to the unit.

Thus, the next larger measure is a length ten times that of the metre, and is called a decametre (Gr. δίκα, *deca*, ten). The next larger measure is a length 100 (that is, 10 × 10) times that of the metre, called a hectometre (Gr. ἑκατόν, *hecaton*, a hundred). The largest measure practically used, is a length of 1000 (that is, 10 × 10 × 10) metres, called a kilometre (Gr. χίλια, *chilia*, a thousand).

Similarly, for the smaller measures, we have a length of $\frac{1}{10}$ of a metre, called a decimetre (Lat. *decem*, ten); a length of $\frac{1}{100}$ of a metre, called a centimetre (Lat. *centum*, a hundred); and a length of $\frac{1}{1000}$ of a metre, called a millimetre (Lat. *mille*, a thousand).

Thus, the names of all the measures larger than the unit, are constructed by adding to the name of the unit a prefix derived from a *Greek* numeral; the names of the measures smaller than the unit, are obtained by adding to the name of the unit a prefix derived from a *Latin* numeral.

A complete table of the measures of Length is given below, and fig. 104 (next page) shows the actual length of a decimetre, which is divided into centimetres and millimetres; a scale of English inches is added for comparison, by which it is seen that a decimetre is very nearly equal to four inches.

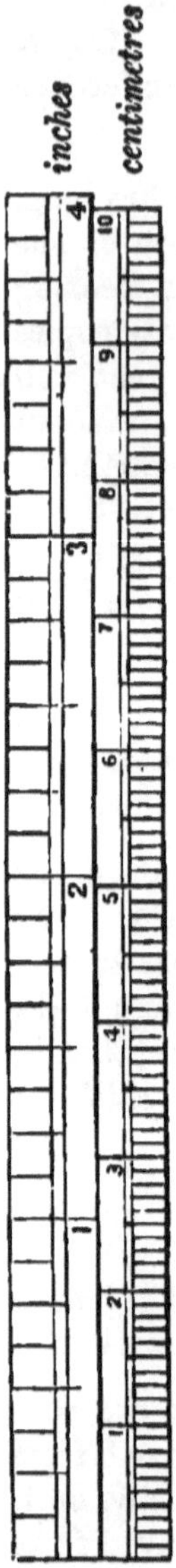

TABLE OF THE MEASURES OF LENGTH.

(The usual abbreviations are put in brackets.)

Kilometre...	=	1000 metres.
Hectometre..	=	100 ,,
Decametre..	=	10 ,,
METRE (m.)..	=	1 metre.
Decimetre..	=	0·1 ,,
Centimetre (cm.).................................	=	0·01 ,,
Millimetre (mm.).................................	=	0·001 ,,

The table may also be put in the following form:

10 millimetres.....................................	=	1 centimetre.
10 centimetres.....................................	=	1 decimetre.
10 decimetres	=	1 metre.
10 metres...	=	1 decametre.
10 decametres.....................................	=	1 hectometre.
10 hectometres...................................	=	1 kilometre.

MEASURES OF VOLUME.

The unit of Volume or capacity, is a cube, each side of which measures 1 decimetre (in other words, 'one cubic decimetre'). It is called a LITRE; and from it the larger and smaller measures of volume are derived in precisely the same way as those of length are derived from the metre. Their names are also given on a similar principle (*Greek* prefixes being used for the larger, *Latin* prefixes for the smaller measures); and the following table hardly requires further explanation.

Fig. 104.

TABLE OF THE MEASURES OF VOLUME.

(The usual abbreviations are put in brackets.)

Kilolitre..	=	1000 litres.
Hectolitre	=	100 ,,
Decalitre..	=	10 ,,
LITRE	=	1 litre.
Decilitre...	=	0·1 ,,
Centilitre...	=	0·01 ,,
Millilitre (or cubic centimetre) (c.c.)...	=	0·001 ,,

It should be noted:

1. That the name 'cubic centimetre' is almost universally used instead of 'millilitre' (a cubic centimetre being readily demonstrated to be $\frac{1}{1000}$ of a cubic decimetre, or litre).

APPENDIX. 161

2. That quantities smaller than the litre are usually expressed in cubic centimetres. Thus three-fourths of a litre would be expressed, not as 7 decilitres 5 centilitres, but as 750 cubic centimetres.

MEASURES OF WEIGHT.

The unit of Weight is the weight of one cubic centimetre (millilitre) of water, at the temperature of 4° centigrade.* It is called a GRAMME, and from it the larger and smaller weights, and their names are derived in exactly the same way as in the case of the measures of length and volume.

TABLE OF WEIGHTS.
(The usual abbreviations are given in brackets.)

Kilogramme.................................	= 1000	grammes.
Hectogramme...............................	= 100	"
Decagramme.................................	= 10	"
GRAMME (grm.)............................	= 1	gramme.
Decigramme..................................	= 0·1	"
Centigramme.................................	= 0·01	"
Milligramme..................................	= 0·001	"

RULES FOR REDUCTION.
(These apply to all the tables given above.)

I. To reduce the larger and smaller measures to the unit, and vice versâ. (Principle.—*The name of each measure expresses what multiple of the unit it is.*)

(a) To reduce a given larger measure to the unit, or a given unit to one of the smaller measures.

Multiply by the number expressed in the name of the measure.

Examples:

Reduce 18 *kilo*metres to metres. 18 × 1000 = 18,000 m.

Reduce 6 grammes to *centi*grammes. 6 × 100 = 600 grms.

(b) To reduce a given smaller measure to the unit, or a given unit to one of the larger measures.

Divide by the number expressed in the name of the measure.

Examples:

Reduce 1885 *centi*metres to metres. 1885 ÷ 100 = 18·85 m.

Reduce 1724 litres to *deca*litres. 1724 ÷ 10 = 172·4 decalitres.

---

* The reason why this particular temperature is specified in defining the gramme is as follows: A given mass of water alters in bulk as its temperature changes (as is more fully explained in treatises on Heat); but at 4° C. it occupies the smallest space that it ever occupies while in the liquid state. Hence a cubic centimetre of water has more matter in it, and therefore weighs more, at 4° C. than at any other temperature.

II. To reduce any given measure to the next larger or the next smaller measure. (Principle.—*Each measure is ten times the next smaller one, and one-tenth of the next larger one.*)

(*a*) To reduce a measure to the next larger one.
Divide the number by 10.
Example: Reduce 152 centigrammes to decigrammes.
$$152 \div 10 = 15\cdot 2 \text{ decigrammes.}$$

(*b*) To reduce a measure to the next smaller one.
Multiply the number by 10.
Example: Reduce 16·2 kilometres to hectometres.
$$16\cdot 2 \times 10 = 162 \text{ hectometres.}$$

It is obvious that, since our system of numeration is, like the metric system itself, a *decimal* system, that is, is based on the number 10, all the processes of multiplication and division required by the above rules are extremely simple. The actual figures have not to be changed at all; their value is altered simply by changing their place in reference to the units-figure. This is, of course, done by altering the position of the decimal point; the latter being always considered to exist, even if not actually expressed, immediately after (that is, to the *right* of) the units-figure.

Thus, to multiply a number by

10, shift the decimal point one place to the *right*.
100, " " two places.
1000, " " three places, &c.

Again, to divide a number by

10, shift the decimal point one place to the *left*.
100, " " two places.
1000, " " three places, &c.

Cyphers being put in, if necessary, to fill up the interval between the decimal point (implied or expressed), and the first figure of the number which is being dealt with.

It will be useful to bear in mind the following points in connection with the metric system :

1. That the number of **cubic decimetres** which expresses the size of a body, also expresses the volume of the body in **litres** (since a cubic decimetre is, by definition, 1 litre).

Thus, if a cistern is 6 decims. long, 4 decims. broad, and 3 decims. deep internally, its size will be $(6 \times 4 \times 3 =)$ 72 cubic decimetres; and its capacity is known at once to be 72 litres.

2. That the number which expresses the volume of a given quan-

tity of water in **cubic centimetres**, also expresses (very nearly) its weight in **grammes**, at ordinary temperature (since the gramme is, by definition, the weight of 1 c.c. of water at 4° C.).

Thus 1000 c.c. of water is known at once to weigh (neglecting the small correction for temperature) 1000 grammes, or 1 kilogramme.

Conversely, of course, a given weight of water in grammes will measure (very nearly) the same number of cubic centimetres.

So that, for instance, if 100 c.c. of water are required for an experiment, and no measures are at hand, it will only be necessary to weigh out 100 grammes in a counterpoised beaker, in order to obtain the quantity required.

Again, a very useful measure may be made from a jar or stout test-tube, by counterpoising it, and weighing into it 1, 5, 10, &c. grammes of water, marking the level of the surface of the liquid with a file or diamond, at each successive weighing.

What has just been said applies to the case of other liquids than water, if a correction is made for any difference in density (for an explanation of this term, see par. 90, p. 36). Thus, if a liquid is twice as heavy as the same volume of water, it is obvious that twice as much of it, that is, 2 grammes, must be weighed out in order to obtain a volume of 1 c.c.

UNITS OF FORCE AND WORK.

The quantities adopted in defining the above units are:

The **centimetre** as unit of length.
The **gramme**   "   "   mass.
The **second**   "   "   time.

The unit of Force is called a **Dyne** (Gr. δύναμις, force). It is—**That amount of Force which, acting for 1 second on a mass of 1 gramme, gives it a velocity of 1 centimetre per second.**

For example—Suppose that a force applied for 1 second to a billiard-ball weighing 110 grms., makes it move 80 cm. per sec. Then the value of this force is (110 × 80 =) 8800 dynes.

The unit of Work is called an **Erg** (Gr. εργον, work). It is—**That amount of work which is done by 1 dyne of force acting through a space of 1 centimetre.**

For example—A skater is pushing a chair before him on the ice with a force of 200 dynes. Then for every metre (= 100 cm.) that the chair moves through, he does (100 × 200 =) 20,000 ergs of work.

(*Examples and Exercises on the Metric System are given on p.* 175.)

QUESTIONS AND EXERCISES.

Chapter I.

1. What is the subject of natural science generally, and of those branches of it called Chemistry and Dynamics in particular? What properties, for instance, of a piece of iron would be examined under these branches, respectively?

2. What is a 'molecule'? What evidence have we that molecules are extremely minute—less than one-millionth of an inch in diameter; How does an 'atom' differ from a molecule?

3. State the chief points of distinction between a solid, a liquid, and a gas. Give examples of each, and show how the same thing can be changed from one state to another. How can we explain the difference between the three states of aggregation of matter?

4. What is meant by saying that matter is 'porous'? Give examples showing, for instance, how liquids and gases can be proved to be porous.

5. Steel is hard, tenacious, and elastic. Explain what these properties mean, and how they may be tested by experiment. Compare glass and lead with steel in respect of the above properties.

6. Define 'force.' How can you tell whether a force has acted or is still acting upon a body? Mention all the forces which are acting (a) on a cricket-ball resting on a table, (b) on a boat rowed against a stream, (c) on a ball thrown upwards by a rider in a circus.

7. Distinguish between the forces of cohesion, adhesion, and gravitation; mentioning cases in which they are all three acting.

8. What is meant by 'capillary attraction'? Mention some common cases of its action, and explain the reason of it.

9. State the law of the variation of gravitation-force with distance.

10. A piece of rock weighs 9 lbs. on the earth's surface—that is, 4000 miles from the centre; if it was taken to a place 12,000 miles from the centre, what would it weigh?

11. A leaden ball is at a distance of 4 yards from another ball, and the attraction of gravitation between them is represented by 8 grains. What will be the amount of attraction when they are placed (a) 16 yards apart, (b) 2 yards apart?

12. Distinguish between the 'weight' and the 'mass' of a body, stating how each is measured. Which of them varies with the place where the body is? Give reasons for this variation in amount.

Chapter II.

13. How can we represent the direction and magnitude of a force in a drawing? A weight of 3 oz. is acted on by a force of 4 oz. pulling it to the left, and by another force of 1 oz. pulling it to the right. Represent these forces accurately in a drawing; and state what forces will be required to produce equilibrium, and in what directions they must be applied.
14. A moving cannon-ball is said to have *momentum*. What does this mean, and what must be known in order that it may be calculated? How would you give a racquet-ball the same momentum as a cricket-ball 8 times as heavy?
15. A cannon-ball weighing 2 lbs. is moving at the rate of 1200 feet per second; and a hammer weighing 10 lbs. is thrown with a velocity of 480 feet per second. Find the momentum of each, and compare them.
16. A cricket-ball weighing ¼ lb. is bowled with a velocity of 12 feet per second, and hit with a velocity of 21 feet per second. Compare its momentum in the two cases.
17. A football weighing ½ lb. is kicked with a force which makes it move 24 feet per second: find its momentum. What velocity must a fives-ball weighing 1 oz. have, in order that its momentum may be the same as that of the football?
18. A man running at the rate of 10 yards per second has a momentum of 4500 (in lbs., feet, and seconds); what must be his weight? A fish weighing 8 lbs. has a momentum of 480 (in lbs., feet, and seconds); what must be its velocity?
19. Mention the most important forces in nature, giving examples of their action. Explain the different methods of ascertaining the magnitude of a force.
20. Distinguish between 'mass,' 'weight,' and 'density.' The mass of the planet Saturn is known to be very much greater than that of our earth, and yet its density is less. Explain this.

Chapter III.

21. Write down clearly the first Law of Motion, and give the three statements into which it may be divided, with one example in illustration of each.
22. A greyhound weighing 30 lbs., and running 35 feet per second, is chasing a hare weighing 7 lbs., and running 30 feet per second.

Compare the momenta of the two, and explain why the hare, although running slower, has a good chance of escape.

23. Explain (*a*) why it is an advantage to run before a jump; (*b*) why it is safest to skate *quickly* over thin ice; (*c*) why the rider may lose his seat when a horse either bolts or refuses a jump.

24. Explain what is meant by 'centrifugal tendency.' Show that it is a consequence of the first Law of Motion, and give reasons for not calling it a force.

25. Centrifugal tendency gets less as the size of the circle in which the body is moving gets larger. What condition is omitted in this statement? Explain why, nevertheless, when a weight placed half-way along the spoke of a wheel is moved to the rim, its centrifugal tendency increases.

26. A stone is being whirled in a sling with a velocity which gives a centrifugal tendency equivalent to 5 lbs. If the velocity is increased to 6 times the rate, how many lbs. must the sling be able to bear, that it may not be broken?

27. What is meant by 'friction,' and what are its causes? By what experiments can it be shown (*a*) that friction varies with the pressure between the surfaces, (*b*) that it does *not* vary with the size of the surfaces if the total pressure between them is unaltered? Can you give any reason for the latter law?

28. The coefficient of friction of iron on iron is $\frac{1}{16}$. Explain exactly what this means. A brake-van weighs 5 tons; if all the wheels were prevented from moving, what force would be required to drag it along the rails?

29. A wooden box weighing 20 lbs. is resting on a board, the coefficient of friction between them being $\frac{1}{16}$. Two weights, one of 3 lbs. and the other of 5 lbs., are pulling it eastward; and three weights, of 6 lbs., 5 lbs., and 4 lbs. respectively, are pulling it westward. In which direction will it move, and with what force?

30. An engine weighs 30 tons, and all its wheels are coupled together and worked by the steam. How many trucks, each weighing 8 tons, could it draw along without the wheels slipping?

31. An iron armour-plate is found to require a force of 7 tons to drag it along the iron floor of the foundry; what must be its weight? Suggest methods for moving it more easily, and give reasons for the advantage gained by each method.

32. In making a brake for a railway train, is it best to make the block of wood or of iron, broad or narrow? If the block is of wood, why does the brake act less powerfully when the wheels are gripped so tightly that they cannot turn round?

QUESTIONS AND EXERCISES.

33. Will it be easier for a horse to draw a cart weighing 1½ ton on a common road, or 2 trucks, each weighing 6 tons, on a railway?
34. Explain exactly what is meant by a 'poundal.'
35. A four-oar weighs, with crew, 1000 lbs. How many poundals of force must each of the crew exert (supposing them all to be of equal strength), in order that 1 second after the start the boat may have a speed of 5 feet per second?
36. A man weighing 160 lbs., sculling in a boat weighing 40 lbs., is exerting a force of 2000 poundals. If 400 poundals are required to overcome friction, how many feet per second will the boat be moving 1 second after the start?
37. Define 'composition of forces,' 'resolution of forces,' 'resultant,' 'component.'
38. In a game of the 'tug-of-war' there were 20 men on one side, each exerting a force of 800 poundals; and 18 men on the other side, each exerting a force of 900 poundals. In which direction will the rope move, and with what force?
39. Explain what is meant by the parallelogram of forces. A cricket-ball is bowled with a force of 4 poundals; it is hit by the bat in a direction at right angles to its course with a force of 8 poundals. Explain fully, with a diagram, the direction it will take, and the force with which it will move.
40. Two forces, of 8 and 15 poundals respectively, act upon a body in directions which are at right angles to one another. Find the magnitude and direction of a third force which would just prevent the body from moving.
41. Two forces, of 9 and 12 poundals respectively, act upon a body. Find their resultant, (a) when they act together in the same direction, (b) when they act in opposite directions, (c) when they act at right angles to one another.
42. A steamer is going westward with a velocity of 12 miles an hour; a north wind is blowing with a force which gives it a speed of 5 miles an hour. Explain with a diagram the actual course and velocity of the ship.
43. A ship, sailing along the coast at the rate of 14 miles an hour (= 20 feet per second), is firing at a town on the shore. The gun is pointed in a direction at right angles to the ship's course, and the shot leaves the gun with a velocity of 800 feet per second. Draw a diagram showing the course it takes.
44. A player at cover-point, running parallel to the line between wickets at the rate of 20 feet per second, fields the ball, and throws it at the wicket with a force which gives it a velocity of 50 feet per second. Draw a diagram showing the direction in which he must aim in order to hit the wicket.

We have here given the magnitude and direction of one force, the magnitude but not the direction of the other, and the direction but not the magnitude of the resultant. Let AB (fig. 105), 20 scale-units long, represent the force applied to the ball by the motion of the player in running. Let AD, of indefinite length, represent the direction of the resultant—that is, the line in which the ball must travel in order to hit the wicket. Round the centre B, with a radius of 50 scale-units, describe an arc of a circle cutting AD in D. Join BD. Through D draw DC parallel to AB, and through A draw AC parallel to BD. Then, if A is the point where the ball leaves the hand, AC is the direction in which it must be thrown in order to hit the wicket.

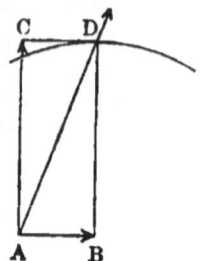

Fig. 105.

PROOF.—ABDC is, by construction, a parallelogram; hence the diagonal AD represents correctly a resultant force equivalent to the two components AC and AB. Now AB, 20 units long, represents the force applied to the ball in consequence of the motion of the player in running. And AC = BD, which latter (being a radius of the circle) is 50 units long. Hence AC represents correctly in magnitude and direction the force with which the player must throw the ball, in order that it may move in the resultant direction AD.

45. Show that, when a boat is towed along a canal by a horse on the bank, it is an advantage to have the towing-rope as long as possible. If the rope is 60 feet long, and the distance from the mast (to which it is fastened) to the bank is 11 feet, calculate what proportion of the force exerted by the horse is effective in dragging the boat straight along the canal.

46. A box weighing 120 lbs. is being drawn along a floor by a rope 13 feet long, attached to it close to the floor, and sloping upwards to the shoulder, 5 feet above the floor. Draw a diagram showing how much of the force applied along the rope is effective in moving the box along the floor. If the coefficient of friction is $\frac{1}{10}$, calculate how much force must be used to drag the box along.

47. Apply the principles of the second Law of Motion to explain (a) the apparent slanting direction of vertically-falling rain-drops when seen from a moving carriage; (b) the spinning of an artificial minnow when dragged through the water; (c) the onward motion of a fish caused by the lateral movement of its tail; (d) the lessening of the useful effect of an oar when it is not at right angles to the length of the boat, or when the blade is not held square to the water; (e) why a windmill works when the axis to which the sails are attached points in the direction of the wind, but not when the axis is at right angles to the wind.

48. What is meant by the 'reaction' which occurs in the application of

a force? Mention some cases of it which you have observed, other than those described in the book.

49. A cannon weighs 600 lbs., and a ball weighing 4 lbs. is shot out of it with a velocity of 1500 feet per second. With what velocity will the gun recoil?
50. A ball is shot out from a cannon with a velocity of 900 feet per second. The cannon weighs 360 lbs., and its velocity at the commencement of the recoil was 5 feet per second. What was the weight of the ball?
51. A fishing-boat weighing 4 tons is lying-to (unanchored) 40 yards from the shore; and a man in it is hauling a cask weighing 2 cwt. from the shore. How far will the cask be from the shore when it is close to the boat?
52. An arrow weighing 4 oz., and moving 176 feet per second, kills a sitting bird weighing 40 oz. With what velocity will the two bodies move on together?
53. An engine weighing 40 tons, and moving 12 miles an hour, strikes a truck weighing 8 tons which is standing on the line. With what velocity will the two move after the collision?
54. A loaded truck, weighing 12 tons, running down an incline, strikes some carriages weighing 18 tons, which are standing at a station. The whole move on at the rate of 12 miles an hour. At what rate was the truck moving when it struck the carriages?
55. A football player, weighing 12 stone and running 10 feet per second, charges another player weighing 10 stone and running in the opposite direction at the rate of 14 feet per second. What will be the result?
56. A fives-court is 26 feet long and 16 feet broad, and a player hits a ball from the middle of the court, in such a direction that it strikes the front wall 4 feet from the left-hand corner. Draw a diagram to scale, showing where the ball will strike the side wall.

Chapter IV.

57. A train starts from a station, and at the end of 1 second is found to be moving at the rate of 2 feet per second. If the acceleration was uniform, what would be its velocity at the end of 8, 12, 16, and 24 seconds?
58. What is meant by saying that gravitation is a force of 32 poundals? Explain fully why it causes all things to fall equally quickly.
59. A bag of sand is let fall from a balloon. Assuming that it falls 16 feet in the first second, show how we can find (a) its velocity at the end of the first second, (b) the space through which it falls

during the third second, (c) the total space it will have fallen through in 7 seconds.

60. A war-rocket is fired point-blank at some men at a distance. It moves through 4 feet in the first second, and reaches its destination in 6 seconds. How far were the men off, and what velocity (approximately) had the rocket when it reached them?

61. A carriage is 'slipped' from a train when it is going 30 miles an hour, and brought to a stop in 2 minutes. How far will it have gone from the place where it was detached from the train?

> Since the carriage was going 30 miles an hour when it was detached, the force applied to it by the engine must be such as to give it a velocity of 1 mile in 2 minutes (taking 2 minutes as the unit of time), if nothing occurred to stop its movement. Now the force necessary to destroy this motion must be equal to the force which produced it. But a force which, applied for 2 minutes, produces a velocity of 1 mile per 2 minutes will (as explained in par. 225, p. 90) make the body move through a space corresponding to the *average* velocity during the time; which is *half* the final velocity, that is, half a mile per 2 minutes. So the carriage would, under the action of such a force, pass through half a mile in the 2 minutes; and this is, therefore, the distance it will traverse before it is stopped.

62. A piece of coal let fall down the shaft of a mine reached the bottom in 9 seconds. How deep was the mine?

63. Explain the cause of the upward motion of an ordinary rocket. Why is it necessary that a stick should be attached to it?

64. A rocket weighing 2 lbs. is driven upwards by a continuous force of 72 poundals. How high will it rise in 4 seconds?

65. The speed of a railway train increases uniformly after starting; and at the end of a minute it has gone 200 yards. Find what velocity in yards per minute it has now gained, and how many yards it will go in the next minute, if the speed goes on increasing at the same rate.

Chapter V.

66. What is meant by the 'centre of gravity'? How does the steadiness with which anything rests on a support depend on the position of the centre of gravity? Give several examples in illustration.

67. A square pillar is 60 feet high and 2 feet square. How would you find out where its centre of gravity was? How would you examine whether it was upright or not? If it was not upright, how would you ascertain whether it was in danger of toppling over?

68. Explain how the centre of gravity of a piece of cardboard may be found (a) if it is triangular, (b) if it is quite irregular in shape. How would you prove the point found to be the true centre of gravity?

QUESTIONS AND EXERCISES 171

69. Explain the exact meaning of the common expressions, 'above,' 'below,' 'keeping one's balance,' 'a well-trimmed boat,' 'top-heavy.'

70. A cylindrical factory chimney, 100 feet high and 3 feet in diameter, leans 2 feet from the perpendicular—that is, so that a plumb-line let fall from the edge of the top on one side touches the ground 2 feet from the edge of the base on that side; how much farther might it lean without actually falling?

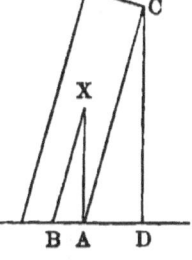

Fig. 106.

Let fig. 106 represent the chimney in such a position that it would be in unstable equilibrium. Since it is cylindrical and uniform in structure, its centre of gravity will be at the middle of its figure, X. From X let fall the perpendicular XA: this will, as explained in par. 246, p. 100, pass through the edge of the base at A. Through X draw XB parallel to the sides of the chimney; B will be the centre of the base, and since the chimney is 3 feet diameter, the distance BA will be 1½ feet.

From the edge of the top at C let fall the perpendicular CD, touching the ground at D. We have to find how far D is from A, the edge of the base.

Now, the triangles XBA and CAD are equiangular, for XB is parallel to CA, and XA to CD, and BA and AD are in the same straight line. Hence (by Eucl. vi. 4) CA : XB :: AD : BA. But CA is twice XB, for X is the middle point of the chimney, therefore AD is twice BA.

But BA is 1½ foot, ∴ AD is 3 feet.

Therefore a plumb-line let fall from C would touch the ground 3 feet from the base of the chimney, when the latter was on the point of toppling over.

71. Explain by the Laws of Equilibrium, (a) why any one in danger of falling stretches out an arm or a leg in the opposite direction; (b) why any one stooping forward advances one foot; (c) why weights are put between the centre and rim of the driving-wheel of an engine, and what must be considered in fixing their mass and position; (d) why a cask will roll down a slope on which a box would rest pretty steadily.

Chapter VI.

72. Define energy, and distinguish between the two forms which it may assume, giving examples of both.

73. What is a 'foot-pound'?

74. A trunk weighing 1½ cwt. is to be carried up-stairs to a room 30 feet above the ground; how many foot-pounds are required?

75. A cricket-ball weighing 5¼ oz. is thrown 20 yards straight up; how many foot-pounds are required?

76. How far could a fives-ball weighing 1 oz. be thrown up by the same muscular power?

77. A cricket-ball weighing ¼ lb. is thrown straight up, and 5 seconds elapse before it returns to the hand. How high did it go, and how many foot-pounds of energy were used in throwing it?

78. The weight used in a pile-driver (see fig. 52, p. 120) is 2 cwt.; and it is raised 6 feet by the efforts of 3 men. How much work does each of them do every time that it is lifted?

79. A battering-ram weighing 1 cwt. is driven against a gate with a velocity of 60 feet per second. What velocity must a cannon-ball weighing 5 lbs. have, in order to have the same energy?

80. A bullet weighing 1 oz. is fired vertically upwards, and rises for 11 seconds before it stops. How high will it rise (neglecting the resistance of the air), and how many foot-pounds of work will it do if it falls on the roof of a house 36 feet high?

81. A train of 40 trucks, each weighing 6 tons, is moving 15 miles an hour; compare its momentum with that of a train of 9 carriages, each weighing 4 tons, moving 50 miles an hour. Compare also the amount of damage each would do in a collision before its motion was stopped.

82. Define 'horse-power,' showing how it differs from work.

83. An engine of 2 horse-power is intended to work a hammer which has to be raised 2 feet high 40 times a minute. What is the utmost weight the hammer can have, allowing 60 foot-pounds for friction, &c.?

84. A machine can raise 12 tons to a height of 10 feet in 2 minutes. Of how many horse-power is it?

85. The depth of a coal-pit is 120 fathoms (a fathom = 6 feet); how many tons of coal will an engine of 3 horse-power raise from the bottom of it per hour?

Chapter VII.

86. What is meant by a 'machine'? A machine cannot do more work than that amount which is applied to it; explain why, nevertheless, a power of 1 lb. can, by means of pulleys, raise a resistance of 8 lbs. (nearly). How many movable pulleys, arranged on the first system, would be required to do this? Give a drawing of the arrangement.

87. Explain the meaning of the term 'mechanical advantage,' and illustrate it by reference to a windlass for raising stones from a quarry. If the mechanical advantage of the windlass is 6, what weight of stone ought a man, exerting a force of 40 lbs., to be able to raise?

Why can he not, in practice, raise quite so much as this by the machine?

88. A bell weighing 1 ton has to be raised to a belfry 30 yards above the ground. How many foot-pounds of work will have to be done? What machine or machines may be used for the purpose? Give a sketch and explanation of an arrangement by which two men, each exerting a force of 120 lbs., can do the work.

89. A bucket of water, weighing 60 lbs., has to be raised from the bottom of a well 20 yards deep by the help of a single movable pulley. What power will be required, and what length of rope will have passed through the man's hands by the time the bucket reaches the top of the well?

90. A man weighing 150 pounds is pulling up a weight of 7 cwt. by means of 3 movable pulleys, arranged on the first system. What is his pressure upon the floor on which he stands?

91. In what respects does the second system of pulleys differ from the first system? Describe the usual form of the second system, and show how the mechanical advantage can be estimated.

92. Four pulleys are given you, one of which is simply for use as a fixed pulley to change the direction in which the power moves. Explain how you would arrange the others, (*a*) on the first system, (*b*) on the second system, so as to get the greatest mechanical advantage. Compare the mechanical advantage obtainable by each arrangement.

93. In a model of a wheel and axle, the diameter of the axle is 3 inches, and a weight of 15 oz. is suspended from it; the diameter of the wheel is 8 inches, and a weight of 6 oz. is suspended from it. Which weight will descend, and with what force will it press upon the floor after reaching it?

94. The handle of a windlass is 2 feet long; the axle is 6 inches diameter. A bucket of water, weighing 80 lbs., has to be raised by means of it; what power is required?

95. A windlass is used for lifting the weight of a 'pile-driver' (fig. 52, p. 120); the handle is 21 inches long, the diameter of the axle is 7 inches. The power available is one of 60 lbs.; how heavy may the weight be? How many turns of the handle will be necessary to raise it to a height of 11 feet?

96. The diameter of a capstan is 10 inches; the length of each capstan-bar measured from the centre is 5 feet; ten men are employed, each exerting a force of 40 lbs. If one-fifth of the whole force is lost by friction, how heavy an anchor can be raised?

97. The wheel of a bicycle is 50 inches diameter; the radius of the treadle is 5 inches; the weight of the rider together with that of

the machine is 240 lbs. What power will be required to move the bicycle along a level road? (Coefficient of friction = $\frac{1}{15}$ of load.)

98. Point out the connection between the wheel and axle and the lever, and show how the mechanical advantage of a lever can be estimated.

99. In a lever of the first order, the power-arm is 30 inches long, the resistance-arm is 2 inches long. What resistance could be moved by a power of 20 lbs.?

100. A fives-ball, hung from one end of a stick 2 feet 6 inches long, is found to balance a cricket-ball hung from the other end, when the stick is supported on a finger placed 5 inches from the cricket-ball. How much heavier is the cricket-ball than the fives-ball?

101. A man wishes to carry two boxes, one weighing 60 lbs., the other weighing 40 lbs., placed one at each end of a pole 5 feet long across his shoulder. At what point must his shoulder be placed?

102. Two men, A and B, are carrying a cask weighing 128 lbs. on a pole 8 feet long laid across their shoulders, the load being 6 inches nearer to A than to B. What share of the burden does each bear?

103. Of what kind of lever is a pair of nut-crackers an example?

104. A nut can just resist a force of 4 lbs., and the outer ends of a pair of nut-crackers 6 inches long are compressed by the hand with a force of 3 lbs. At what point must the nut be placed so as just to crack?

105. A ladder, uniform in breadth and structure, is being raised from a horizontal to a vertical position, the lower end being held steadily down. (1) Find the position and path of its centre of gravity. (2) State what orders of levers it represents during its rise. (3) Explain why the work becomes easier when the ladder is nearly vertical.

106. The distance from the middle of the blade of an oar (where the fulcrum may be considered to be applied) to the rowlock is 8 feet; the distance from the rowlock to the point where the rower's force is applied is 3 feet. The rower exerts a force of 56 poundals; what is the actual force urging the boat on? Why does this force vary in different parts of the stroke, and in what position of the oar is it the greatest?

107. A carriage weighing 2 tons has to be drawn by a horse up an incline of 1 in 40. What power is required? (Coefficient of friction = $\frac{1}{15}$.)

108. A train of 28 trucks, each weighing 8 tons, has to be dragged up an incline of 1 in 90, by an engine capable of exerting a tractive force of 3 tons. Can the engine do the work? (Coefficient of friction = $\frac{1}{180}$.)

109. The pitch of the screw of a screw-press is 1 inch; the length of the handle by which it is turned is 21 inches. If a power of 10 lbs. is applied to the end of the handle, what force will be available for compression (20 per cent. being allowed for loss by friction)?

EXERCISES ON THE METRIC SYSTEM.

1. Reduce 1886 millimetres to the decimal fraction of a metre.
2. How many centimetres are there in 15·35 metres?
3. How many metres are there in 39,371 millimetres?
4. Express 48 kilometres, 3 hectometres, 1 decametre, in metres.
5. How many kilometres are there in 3,675,824 millimetres?
6. The length of a cricket-bat is 86 centimetres; the distance between wickets is 20·21 metres. How many bats' lengths is this?
7. A ladder is 6·6 metres long; the distance between the rungs is 22 centimetres; how many rungs are there?
8. The driving-wheel of a locomotive is 5 metres 2 decimetres in circumference. How many kilometres will it pass over in turning round 500 times?
9. How many litres are there in a cubic metre?
10. A cistern is 8 decimetres long, 5 decimetres broad, and 6 decimetres deep. How many litres will it hold?
11. A trough is 2·4 metres long, 6 decimetres broad, and 120 millimetres deep. How many litres will it hold?
12. A lecture room is 9 metres long, 7 metres broad, and 5 metres high. How many litres of air does it contain?
13. What is the weight of (*a*) a litre of water; (*b*) a cubic metre of water, in kilogrammes, and in hectogrammes?
14. How many litres will 8 kilogrammes, 3 hectogrammes, of water measure?
15. A cistern is 2·2 metres long, 90 centimetres broad, and 1·2 metres deep. How many litres of water will it hold, and what will the water weigh?
16. 24 centilitres of water are required for an experiment, but no measures are at hand. What quantity of water must be weighed out in order to get this volume?

17. If you had a long narrow tube closed at one end (a 'test-tube'), scales and weights, and some water, explain how you would graduate the tube as a measure of cubic centimetres.

18. A rifle bullet, weighing 30 grammes, is shot with a velocity of 400 metres per second out of a rifle weighing 4·2 kilogrammes. Find the momentum of the bullet (in centimetre-gramme-seconds), and the velocity in centimetres per second with which the rifle recoils.

19. When a mass of 1 gramme is allowed to fall freely under the action of gravitation, at the end of 1 second it has fallen through 490 centimetres, and has acquired a velocity of 980 centimetres. What is the value of gravitation-force in dynes, and how many ergs of work will the mass do if it strikes the ground at the end of the first second?

20. A racquet-ball weighing 18 grammes is driven with a force which gives it a velocity of 40 metres per second. Express its kinetic energy in ergs.

INDEX.

	PAGE
'Above,' meaning of term	31
Acceleration, meaning of term	87
" " produced by Gravitation	88
Adhesion, meaning of	21
'Arms' of a lever, meaning of	141
Atoms, account of	12
Attraction, various kinds of	15
Balance, or pair of scales, description of	143
Ballast in a ship, use of	104
Barge, action of forces upon a	74
'Below' meaning of term	31
Bicycle, description of	138
Bicycles, ball-bearings for	64
Biology, definition of	6
Brittleness, meaning of	18
Bullet, danger of firing upwards a	95
" energy of, compared with that of the rifle	119
Cannon, recoil of	79
" ball, energy of	119
" " momentum of	41
Capillarity, meaning of	24
Capstan, description of	137
Cause and Effect	5
Centre of Gravity, meaning of term	95
" " methods of finding	106–110
Centre of Inertia	110
Centre of Percussion	110
Centrifugal extractor	54
Centrifugal tendency, effect of, on weight	34, 56
Centrifugal tendency, illustrations of	53
" " laws of	51

	PAGE
Centrifugal tendency, meaning of	50
" " orbits of the planets influenced by	56
Chemistry, definition of	6
Cohesion-figures	24
Cohesion, general account of	16
" overcome by heat	17
Coining Press, the	154
Collision of bodies	80
Colloids	27
Component forces, meaning of	68
Composition of Forces	68
Cone, made to balance on its point	104
Conservation of Energy	115
Cricket-ball, action of forces upon a	72
Cricket-bat, as a lever of the Third Order	148
Cricket-bat, centre of percussion of a	111
" " stinging of a, explained	111
Crown glass, manufacture of	54
Crystalloids	27
'Degradation' of Energy	157
Densities, relative, table of	37
Density, meaning of	36
Dialysis, operation of	28
Diffusion of gases	27
" of liquids	27
Divisibility of matter	11
'Doubling' by hares, principle of	48
Ductility	19
Dynamics, definition of	7
'Dyne,' the, defined	163
Earth, attraction of	29, 95
" movements of the	55, 56
" reasons for shape of the	56

ELEMENTARY DYNAMICS.

	PAGE
Elastic bodies, collision of	82
Elasticity, meaning of	20
Elbow-joint, description of the	147
Energy of the Sun	114
" conservation of	115
" 'degradation' of	157
" exact valuation of	121
" meaning of	111
" measurement of	116
" relation of, to velocity	118
" statical and kinetic	112–114
" transference of	112
Equilibrium, different kinds of	98
" examples of	99
" experiments illustrating	97
" laws of	100–104
" of forces	41
" of bodies	96
'Erg,' the, defined	163
Extension and Form	8
Falling bodies, experiments illustrating laws of	88–90
Falling bodies, table of spaces passed through by	92
Falling bodies, work done by	119
Ferry-boat, action of forces upon a	72
First Law of Motion	45
Fives-ball, mode of calculating the direction in which to hit a	86
'Foot-pound,' meaning of	117
Force, meaning of term	39
" metric units of	163
" moment of a	143
" unit of	66
Forces, composition of	68
" continued action of	87
" direction of, mode of expressing	40
Forces, equilibrium of	41
" examples of	40
" independent action of	67
" magnitude of, mode of expressing	40
Forces, measurement of	42
" parallelogram of	71
" resolution of	73
Friction, advantages and disadvantages of	64
Friction, causes of	57
" coefficient of	61

	PAGE
Friction, coefficient of, on roads and railways	62
Friction, laws of	57–61
" meaning of	57
" methods of lessening	61
" rolling, nature of	63
" table of coefficients of	61
" variation of, with pressure	59
Friction-wheels	64
Fulcrum, meaning of	141
Gaseous state, definition of	10
Gases, diffusion of	27
" elasticity of	21
" kinetic theory of	17
" porosity of	14
" table of densities of	37
Glass, elasticity of	21
'Gradient' of a road, explained	150
Gravitation, general account of	29
" action of, in acceleration	88
" law of variation with distance	33
Gravity, centre of, meaning of term	95
Hardness, list of substances in order of	18
Hardness, meaning of	18
Heaviness, meaning of	29
Height of a tower, method of finding	92
" to which a ball has risen, method of finding	94
'Horse-power,' meaning of term	120
Impenetrability	8
Incidence, angle of	84
Inclined Plane	148–154
Indestructibility of matter	13
Inertia, centre of	110
" examples of	45–49
" meaning of	45
Irregular bodies, method of finding the centre of gravity of	109
Isochronism of the pendulum	123
Kinetic Energy	113
" theory of gases	17
Kinetics, methods employed in	42
Law of nature	6
Laws of centrifugal tendency	51–54

INDEX. 179

	PAGE
Laws of equilibrium	100–104
" falling bodies	88–90
" friction	57–60
" motion	44
" reflexion	83
Leaning towers	101
Levers	140–148
" different orders of	141
Liquid state, definition of	10
Liquids, table of densities of	37
Locomotive engine, the	154–157
Machines, definition of	128
" different classes of	131
Magnitude and direction of forces	40
Malleability	19
Mass, meaning of	35
" and Weight, distinction between	35
Matter, definition of	7
" divisibility of	11
" indestructibility of	13
" porosity of	14
" properties of	7
" the three states of	9
'Mechanical advantage,' general method of calculating	130
'Mechanical advantage,' meaning of	130
Metals, porosity of	14
Metric System, the	158
" " rules for reduction in	161
" " units of force and work in	163
Molecules, account of	12
Moment of a force	143
Momentum, meaning of term	41
" method of expressing	41
" problems on	43
Motion, laws of	44
" meaning of term	38
Movable pulleys	132
Natural Science, branches of	6
Nature, laws of	6
Neutral equilibrium	98
Newton, Sir Isaac, his laws of motion	44
" " investigation of gravitation by	30
Non-elastic bodies, collision of	81
Oar, principle of action of an	145
Osmose, meaning of	28

	PAGE
Paper, method of splitting a sheet of	22
Parallelogram of forces	71
Pendulum, account of the	122–127
" length of the seconds	125
'Perpetual Motion,' impossibility of	116
Physics, definition of	7
'Pile-driver,' description of a	120
Pisa, leaning tower of	102
Plumb-line	30
Porosity of Matter	14
Potential (statical) Energy	113
Poundal	66
'Power' in machines, meaning of	128
'Preserving one's balance,' meaning of term	102
Pulleys, fixed and movable	131
" systems of	133–135
Questions and Exercises	164–176
Rack and Pinion, description of	137
Reaction of a force, meaning of	77
Recoil of a gun, explanation of	79
Reflexion, angle of	84
" laws of	83
'Resistance' in machines, meaning of	128
Resolution of Forces	73
Resultant force, meaning of	68
Rifle, recoil of a	79
Rocket, ascent of a, explained	80
Rod, method of finding the centre of gravity of a	106
Rowing, use of the stretcher in	80
Rudder, action of a	76
Running before a jump, principle of	48
Screws	152–154
Second Law of Motion	65
Skating, theory of	102
Slinging a stone, principle of	53
Softness, meaning of	18
Solid state, definition of	10
Solids, table of densities of	37
Specific gravities, table of	37
Spring-balance, principle of	32
Stable equilibrium	98
States of Aggregation	9
Statical Energy	113
Statics, methods employed in	42
Steel, hardening and tempering of	21
Steelyard, description of	144

	PAGE
Stretcher in rowing, use of a	80
Sun, the, as a source of energy	114
Surface tension of liquids	23
Swing, theory of setting in motion a	105
Tenacity, meaning of	19
Third Law of Motion	77
Throwing a ball, principle of	49
″ the hammer, principle of	53
'Top-heavy,' meaning of term	98
Tossing oars, risk of upsetting in	104
Train of wheels and pinions	139
Tug of War, the game of	69
Unit of work	117
Unstable equilibrium	98
Velocity, meaning of term	39

	PAGE
Viscosity	17
Water, falling, as a source of energy	114
Wedges	151
'Weighing' things, meaning of	144
″ ″ methods of	31
Weight, meaning of	29
″ reasons for difference of	34
″ and Mass, distinction between	35
Wheel and Axle	135–140
Whirling-table, description of	51
Windlass, description of	137
Wire-drawing	20
Work, meaning of	111
″ metric unit of	163
″ relation of, to time	120
″ table of different kinds of	121
″ unit of	117

THE END.

Edinburgh:
Printed by W. & R. Chambers.

www.ingramcontent.com/pod-product-compliance
Lightning Source LLC
Chambersburg PA
CBHW032151160426
43197CB00008B/862